Overleaf: Tweed Memorial Park in spring

THE *Apple*

A HISTORY OF CANADA'S PERFECT FRUIT

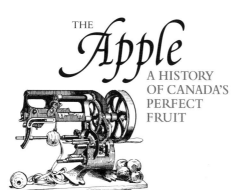

THE Apple

A HISTORY OF CANADA'S PERFECT FRUIT

Carol Martin

McArthur & Company
Toronto

First published in Canada in 2007
McArthur & Company
322 King Street West, Suite 402
Toronto, ON, M5V 1J2
www.mcarthur-co.com

Library and Archives Canada Cataloguing in Publication

Martin, Carol, 1955–
   The apple : a history of Canada's perfect fruit / Carol Martin.

ISBN 978-1-55278-679-6

1. Apples--Canada--History. 2. Apples--History. I. Title.

SB363.2.C2M38 2007   634'.110971   C2007-905085-9

Design: Miriam Bloom, Expression Communications Inc.
Index: Elaine Melnick
Printed in Canada by Transcontinental

The publisher would like to acknowledge the financial support of the Government of Canada through the Book Publishing Industry Development Program (BPIDIP) and the Canada Council for our publishing activities. The publisher further wishes to acknowledge the financial support of the Ontario Arts Council for our publishing program.

10 9 8 7 6 5 4 3 2 1

TO MY BROTHER,

FRANK WOOD,

WHO RESEARCHED APPLES IN THE OKANAGAN FOR ME

CONTENTS

ACKNOWLEDGEMENTS

Over the past few years, I have spent many hours of research in libraries, archives and in the field for my previous projects – an exhibition at Library and Archives Canada on "Cultivating Canadian Gardens" and a book on *A History of Canadian Gardening*. As I spoke to people and read the history, I often came across interesting stories about apples: Champlain referring to the "little wild apples" during his early exploration of North America, and a few years later bringing young saplings to Quebec to establish North America's first culti-vated orchard; the early settlers planting orchards as soon as a little land was cleared; the later impor-tance of trade in apples with Europe; the changes over the years in the apples grown, the care of the trees and the ups and downs on the business side; the omnipresence of the apple today and how we benefit from its beauty, its sweetness and its valuable nutrients. It seemed we were not paying enough atten-tion to this wonderful fruit and to its significance in the Canadian story and that someone should devote a book to it. I decide to take on that task.

It has been a fascinating study and my time spent with growers and distributors, and in libraries and archives, has been well rewarded.

I have many people to thank for helping me along the way. Many men and women welcomed me into their offices or homes and told me family stories from the orchard that went back through the generations. They are proud of their history with apples and speak fondly of the struggles of their parents, grandparents and even great-grandparents, and of what they are now doing to continue to make the growing of apples sustainable in what has become a tough market. The scientists and botanists spoke and wrote of the ongoing research in breeding, always looking for the elusive perfect apple. The distributors acknowledged the constant challenge of actually getting apples into the hands of buyers.

I am grateful to many in Nova Scotia, in particular to Charles Embree of the Atlantic Food and Horticultural Centre at Kentville in the Annapolis Valley who gave me apples to taste, showed me around the centre and the Blair House museum, and introduced me to local growers and others in the field. I want to thank Paul Elderkin who told me his family's apple story, Bill Livingstone of Sarsfield Foods Ltd., David Parrish at Scotian Gold and Jason Dukeshire at the Prescott House Museum.

In New Brunswick, special thanks to Bob Osborne at Cornhill Nursery for the conversation and instructive tour. Dr. Shahrokh Khanizadeh at the Agriculture and Agri-Food plant-breeding station in St-Jean-sur-Richelieu, Quebec, was helpful in many, many ways, for which I thank him.

In Ontario, Shelly Paulocik of Woodwinds Nursery, Dianne Campbell of Campbell's Orchards, Brad Johnston of Barbette Orchards, Ed Laithwaite of Apple Park Farm Market, Grace Lambe of Grandma Lambe's and Ivan McClymont of McClymont Orchard were all kind enough to meet with me and share their stories.

Closer to home in southern Ontario, Joe Reeve of Golden Bough Nursery, Philip Kennedy of Arbour Gardens, Jim Hughes of Hughes Orchards, the late Henry Gray of Hobby Orchard and

Margaret Appleby of the Ontario Ministry of Agriculture, Food and Rural Affairs all gave me their time and interest.

The Davison family of Davison Orchards in Vernon, British Columbia, helped in every way – with information, photographs, books and friendship. They have my gratitude.

Dr. Barrie Juniper of the University of Oxford kindly helped me make my way through the intricacies of early apple history and read the first chapter. Dr. John Proctor, professor emeritus, University of Guelph, gave me much advice and read the manuscript in its final stages as did my good friend, Janet Lunn, who offered useful suggestions.

My thanks to the many friends who have given me support, encouragement and sometimes a bed as I travelled, in particular Miriam and Victor Rabinovitch, Pat Dacey, Michael and Fran Preston and Bill and Jocelyn Smyth.

My family has always been ready to help me with encouragement and interest, my brothers Donald and Frank Wood, and my children Pamela Martin (always available to rescue me when the computer foiled my efforts), Christopher looking over my shoulder with intelligent interest, and Jeremy and his companion Chanel St. Pierre who saved me with the gift of a computer upgrade.

The archives, libraries and individuals who helped me find and allowed me to use the illustrations are acknowledged with the material. I am grateful to them. Unacknowledged photographs are by the author with the exception of a few individual apple photographs which are courtesy of Robert McClelland, Agriculture and Agri-Food Canada. Every effort has been made to contact copyright holders, but if any has been overlooked, corrections will be made in future editions. 🍎

Adam and Eve, 1526 (panel) by Lucas Cranach, the Elder (1472–1553), Samuel Courtauld Trust, Bridgeman Art Library, COU 470

1
IN THE BEGINNING

Apple Dumplings

Make a good puff-paste, pare some large apples, cut them in quarters, and take out the cores very nicely; take a piece of crust, and roll it round, enough for one apple; if they are big, they will not look pretty, so roll the crust round each apple, and make them round like a ball, with a little flour in your hand. Have a pot of water boiling, take a clean cloth, dip it in the water, and shake flour over it; tie each dumpling by itself, and put them in the water boiling, which keep boiling all the time; and if your crust is light and good, and the apples not too large, half an hour will boil them, but if the apples be large, they will take an hour's boiling. When they are enough, take them up, and lay them in a dish; throw fine sugar all over them, and send them to table. Have a good fresh butter melted in a cup, and fine beaten sugar in a saucer.

Mrs. Glasse. *The Art of Cookery Made Plain and Easy*. England: 1747, p. 111.

ALMA ATA, "FATHER OF APPLES"

IN FAR-OFF KAZAKHSTAN in central Asia stands a tall, closed-canopy forest of apple trees of every size and shape. Centuries ago the forest stretched for many kilometres in every direction. Imagine wandering beneath these trees in ancient times, where not only apples, but also pears, cherries and apricots flowered in profusion. This is the birthplace of many of the tree fruits we know today. They were not much like our present-day, sweet, luscious varieties, but in their seeds were stored the genetic possibilities for what would one day become our favourite fruits.

Now, only a tiny percentage of these once great forests remain, but a wide variety of apples still grow there near the city of Almaty (originally Alma Ata, "Father of Apples") on the slopes of Tien Shan, the Heavenly Mountains. Here, in a beautiful setting below snow-capped mountains, each tree is unique and bears its own unique fruit. Many of the apples (*Malus sieversii*) are small and sour, but some are larger and sweeter – closer to our modern domestic apple (*Malus x domestica*). The story of how apples travelled

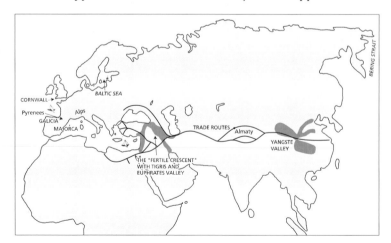

Prehistoric trade routes passed through Kazakhstan and the Almaty region, where many of the earliest apples would have been found.

Elanor McBay, The Drawing Office, Department of Geography, University College, London

2

Young Kazakhstan forest springing
up at the base of the limestone
cliffs of the Tien Shan

Photograph by Barrie Juniper

3

Wild apples from the forests of Kazakhstan, gathered by Barrie E. Juniper in a single day, showing the wide variety still growing there today

Photograph by Barrie Juniper

so far, over such a long period of time, is a tale worthy of the *Arabian Nights*.[1]

Kazakhstan lies to the north and east of the Caspian Sea and stretches as far as China. (There is some evidence that the very earliest fruit trees [*Malus baccata*] were, in fact, to be found in the Gansu Province of northern China more than 10 million years ago.) Kazakhstan has had a troubled and complex history over the centuries, with power shifting back and forth among the

4

region's nomadic tribes. Finally, in 1731, the region was taken over by Russia and later became part of the Soviet Union until gaining independence in 1991 after the breakup of the USSR. North Americans have become more familiar with the country post–9/11 when, because of its proximity to Afghanistan, Kazakhstan was in the news. It is a large country, larger than Ontario and Quebec combined, with about the same, sparse population.

The travel writer Viktor Vitkovich described a visit to Tien Shan in 1960:

> a marvellous garden of wonders such as are described in fairy tales ... where apples and pears look down on you from the trees and beg to be eaten, where a magic wind brings you showers of nuts, where birds are radiantly feathered and animals trustful and the imprints of bears' paws are to be seen on the paths.[2]

Over the centuries, the seeds of the Kazakhstan apples were carried by birds and animals farther east and west until wild crabapples could be found throughout much of Asia and Europe. One theory has it that horses, famous in the history of the area, travelling the ancient network of the trading routes we know as the Silk Route, snacked on the apples and expelled the indigestible seeds as they made their way along the trails some four thousand years ago. Sometime later, other crabapples (*Malus prunifolia*) spread north and east to Russia and China.

The search for the original home of tree fruit has developed slowly over the past century. The renowned Russian botanist and geneticist Nikolai I. Vavilov theorized that the origin of cultivated plants would be found in those regions where they exist in the wilds in the greatest diversity. As early as 1930 he suggested that

The cultivated apple we know today is the species *Malus domestica*, a member of the Rosaceae or rose family. Its seeds, as with all apples, contain a complex genetic structure. In addition, pollen from a second tree is required for germination. As a result, apple trees, like many other plants (and, of course people), do not breed true. That is, every seed of every apple (pome), if successfully grown, will result in a tree or fruit unlike the parent plant. For this reason, an infinite variety of apples is possible. Most of these self-seeded trees bear small sour fruit like the crabapple. However, in spite of attempts of botanists to breed the perfect apple, many, perhaps most, of our favourites are from accidental seedlings (pippins). Apples officially named, recorded and reproduced by grafting are called "cultivars," of which there are thousands.

The carpel or core of an apple always has a beautiful star shape with five seed chambers each containing two dark brown seeds (if the flower has been fully pollinated).

Photograph by Pamela Martin

for apples this would be *M. sieversii* in the Caucasus. Vavilov died in prison in 1943 (a victim of the notorious Lysenko, whose idea that acquired characteristics could be inherited set back Russian biology for decades) and it wasn't until 1989, when Russia opened its doors to outside botanists, that his theories could be explored. Since then, expeditions from Cornell in the United States and Oxford in England have visited the region of the Caucasus to collect the genetic wealth to be found there and, of course, to look for the means to produce the perfect apple. Vavilov was active in the founding of the science of genetics. He is now considered the most distinguished plant breeder of his generation. The Vavilov

Institute of Plant Industry in St. Petersburg still contains the world's largest collection of plant genetic material in the world.

We know that the European wild crabapples (*Malus silvestris*), small, hard and sour though they may have been, were gathered and eaten by early peoples. The remains of this fruit have been discovered in prehistoric sites in Denmark, Switzerland and Yugoslavia. Since wild crabs (*Malus coronaria*) are also native to North America, they may have crossed from Siberia with the early immigrants who trekked over the Bering Land Bridge as early as twenty thousand years ago. Or, perhaps, in a far earlier period, the seeds of primitive fruit were carried by continental drift, when the land masses that became North America and Europe inched apart infinitely slowly. We may never know which theory is closest to the truth.

THE GREEKS AND ROMANS

Apples were very popular with the early Greeks who carefully bred and nurtured them to improve the flavour. Sugar had not yet become available and all fruits were prized for their sweetness. Fruit orchards had become common by this time, and it was already known that apples were self-incompatible and required the pollen from another tree to be fertilized – each new tree and its fruit would be somewhat different from the parent plants. In order to duplicate the fruit of a particularly desirable apple, growers of the period had already learned to bud or graft branches from favourite apple trees to the root or branch of a sturdy tree with less desirable fruit. In 323 BCE, the Greek philosopher Theophrastus described the value of grafting and budding apple trees in his treatise on plants in which he refers to six varieties by name. Therefore, although trees grown from seeds or pips have continued to be nurtured over the years, it has been known for centuries that

The Greeks and Romans were adept at grafting and budding apples to produce the best varieties for the table. This scene illustrating work in the orchard is taken from a Roman floor mosaic, circa the third century CE.

Réunion des Musées Nationaux/
Art Resource, NY

Musée des Antiquités Nationales,
Saint-Germain-en-Laye, France

grafting is the only way to reproduce a branch or tree that will have apples identical to the original.

Later the Romans too became masters at cultivating apple orchards. It isn't clear when the early term usually translated as "apple" actually referred to what we call an apple or when it was used to refer to a wider range of tree fruits. For a long time, apples and pears may have both been referred to as apples since they share so many characteristics.

The poet Horace called Italy one big fruit orchard and noted that the perfect meal ended with apples. And Cicero, in 50 BCE, urged Romans to save their apple seeds to develop new varieties. In 77 CE, Pliny the Elder, in his *Historia Naturalis*, described the popular apples of the day. He also recommended the best way to graft desirable varieties and advocated growing stock from seed to use as roots. His suggestions for storing apples included spacing the apples in dry rooms, with windows that could be opened on suitable days to allow for air circulation; or burying them in sand-filled pits – methods that remained in use for centuries. By the fourth century the Romans were drinking cider made from apples and perry made from pears.

When the Romans settled in Britain and France in the first century BCE, it is assumed that apple trees, which had become so popular with them, were brought along, although no records of this have been discovered. In 410 CE the Romans left Britain followed by a long period of foreign invasions. Information on the cultivation of apples over the next fifteen hundred years is sketchy at best, but the prosperous religious houses that flourished during this time were famous for their gardens and orchards and remained so until the dissolution of the monasteries in England in the 1530s.

Pomme d'Api
This is the oldest apple variety known today. Small, sweet and juicy, it is called the Lady apple in English and is believed to go back to Roman times.
S. Khanizadeh, "Our Apples," www.cyberfruit.info

FRANCE

The Romans were sophisticated gardeners who were adept at grafting; however, their skills were lost over time so that for many centuries this information was not commonly available in much of Europe, probably until the Islamic invasions made it more widespread. Eventually, grafting for valued varieties came into common practice, and some of the apples of earlier times were retained and cultivated. The oldest variety still being grown today is the Lady apple or pomme d'Api, named after the Etruscan grower who is believed to have developed it. A small but delicious eating apple, it was a special favourite of Louis IV.

In France, apples were most popular as dessert at the end of a meal, and cultivars that could be enjoyed raw were encouraged. French gardeners were ingenious in their methods. They trained apples to *espaliers* or trellises and pruned the branches to concentrate on the production of large, perfect fruit. They also discovered how to dwarf trees, producing full crops on small, easily managed plants.

In *The Manner of Ordering Fruit Trees* (published originally in French but translated into English in 1660), Sieur le Gendre described the practice, which seemed to be well established in France by that time. "The best Plant to graffe such apple trees upon as you would have to grow against a wall, in Pallisades or Hedges, and such as you desire to keep low for dwarf trees is that of the Paradise (a kind of codling) apple tree, which grows but little into wood, bears quickly and much fruit."[3]

In Normandy, cider was the most important product of the apple, and the country was famous for its fine cider and Calvados (a distilled cider). There, apple trees were allowed to develop in their own way, each tree different from the other, making for good cider blends. The popularity of Normandy cider rose and fell over the centuries as production was affected by taxes and

Photograph by
Peggy deWitt, Picton

The apple features in many legends and stories – from the Goddess Pomona, protector of fruit trees, to Atalanta and the three golden apples, to William Tell. But the most powerful story is that of Adam and Eve in the Garden of Eden (although it is exceedingly doubtful that the fruit referred to was actually an apple).

Adam and Eve, 1526 (panel) by Lucas Cranach, the Elder (1472–1553), Samuel Courtauld Trust, Bridgeman Art Library, COU 470

government policy; however, it was by far the most common beverage there from the fourteenth century right up to the beginning of the twentieth. After that, French policy discouraged the cultivation of orchards, supporting instead the cultivation of grapes and the production of wine.

THE FRUITERERS SECRETS

By the thirteenth century, records of the kinds of apples grown in England begin to appear. Among them, the most popular seem to have been the Pearman (believed to be the first named variety in English history), which was a favourite dessert apple for the next five hundred years, and the Costard, which was more often used in cooking, particularly in pies. The Costard remained in use up to the time of Shakespeare and its name has been preserved in the word "costermonger" to refer to street vendors selling apples from stalls or barrows.

Writing in 1629, the apothecary John Parkinson described the various uses of apples:

> The best sorts of Apples serve at the last course for the table, in most mens houses of account; where if there grow any rare or excellent fruit, it is then set forth to be seene and tasted.
>
> Divers other sorts serve to bake, either for the Masters Table or the meynes sustenance, either in pyes or pans, or else stewed in dishes with Rosewater and Sugar and Cinnaman or Ginger cast upon.
>
> Some kinds are fittest to roast in the winter time, to warme a cup of wine, ale or beere, or to be eaten alone, for the nature of some fruit is never so good or worth the eating, as when they are roasted.
>
> Some sorts are fitted to scald for codlins and are taken to coole the stomache, as well as to please the taste, having Rosewater and Sugar put to them.
>
> Some sorts are best to make Cider of as in the West Countrey of England great quantities, yea many hogsheads and Tunnes full are made, especially to be carried to the Sea in long voyages: and it is found by experience to be of excellent use to mix with water for beverage. It is usually seen that those fruits that are neither fit to eate raw, roasted nor baked, are fittest for cider and make the best.
>
> The juice of Apples, likewise as of pippins and pearmains, is of good use in Melancholic diseases, helping to produce mirth and to expel heaviness.
>
> The distilled water of the same apples is of like effect.[4]

13

Apple orchards and the interest in serving and nurturing apples expanded rapidly in sixteenth-century England. The *Boke of Husbandry* by Sir Anthony Fitzherbert was the first horticultural publication published in that country. In it he described the grafting of fruit trees and the use of crabapple trees as rootstocks. But it is Richard Harris, fruiterer to Henry VIII, who has been credited with making England a major apple-producing nation. Although apple trees had been imported much earlier from Normandy, they were probably ungrafted and not of dependable quality. In order to supply the court, Harris imported new grafts from France and Belgium, creating an orchard at Newgarden that became a gardening showplace. From these trees, according to *The Fruiterers Secrets* published in 1604, the future orchards of the country were created:

> One Richard Harris borne in Ireland, Fruiterer to King Henry VIII, fetched out of France great store of graftes, especially pippins, before which time there was no right pippins in England ... whereof he made an orchard, planting therein all those foreign grafts. Which orchard is, and hath been from time to time, the chiefe Mother of all other orchards for those kindes of fruits in Kent and of divers other places. ... Gentlemen and others taking delight in grafting (being a matter so necessary and beneficial in a Commonwealth) have planted many orchards; fetching these grafts out of that orchard which Harris planted called Newgarden.[5]

In spite of this, grafting did not really catch on in England for several more centuries and the country therefore lagged behind in producing named varieties of high quality.

Photograph by
Peggy deWitt, Picton

Fresh fruit had originally suffered from a period in which it was held in suspicion by the English, but by the seventeenth century it was increasingly popular. Jellies, tarts, jams and butters were frequent table treats by then. Cider, too, became important in home production and remained so until the middle of the eighteenth century when competition from wine and beer made it expensive, especially when a government tax was applied in 1763. As beer became increasingly popular, it was more economical for the small grower to replace the personal orchard with a crop of hops.

Around this time, imports, first from France and later from North America, began to create a market for new varieties of apples. The most popular varieties in England in the first half of the nineteenth century included Ribston, Court of Wyck Pippin, Duchess of Oldenburg, Old and Scarlet Nonpareil, Golden Pippin, Golden Reinette, King of the Pippins and Wellington for dessert apples; Beauty of Kent, Kentish Codlin, Keswick Codlin, Lemon Pippin and Blenheim Orange for cooking. Apples introduced then

15

In the 1830s, Richard Cox retired with his household to Colnbrook Lawn in Bucks County, England, where he devoted himself to gardening. One of the stories about his remarkable success with apples is that he planted two pippins (seeds) of a Ribston apple in a pot. With incredible luck these developed into two notable apple trees, Cox's Pomona and Cox's Orange Pippin. The latter was to become famous as a crisp, juicy apple with a wide variety of uses. In 1964 it was still listed as the most popular dessert apple in England.

Archival and Special Collections,
McLaughlin Library, University of Guelph

that have remained popular right up to the present are Bramley's Seedling, Cox's Orange Pippin, Lord Derby and Worcester Pearmain. Most of these were chance seedlings.

In 1964, F.A. Roach, writing in the *Journal of the Royal Agricultural Society of England*, summed up the country's apple history in this way: "The whole history of our apple production since the sixteenth century has been one of periodic encouragement and effort on the part of certain far sighted individuals to improve our orchards, both as regards the varieties and quality of apples grown, in order to replace foreign imports. For one brief spell we actually exported a few apples."

In the first part of the seventeenth century, eating apples made their way from Europe to North America by way of the early settlers. ☙

Canadian Illustrated News, 1880 (1970.228). Stewart Museum, Montreal (Canada)

2

THE ORCHARDS OF NEW FRANCE AND QUEBEC

Croquants aux Pommes

*"An old recipe from Quebec. Almost like a bonbon.
Serve as is, or with ice cream."*

Peel, core, and slice 2 large apples. Place in a bowl
with ½ cup chopped nuts. Beat 1 egg with 1 cup
sugar until well beaten to partly dissolve the sugar.
Add 2 tbsp. flour and 1 tsp. baking powder, and
⅛ tsp. salt. Pour into a 9-inch pie plate. Bake 35
minutes in a 375°F oven, or until top is browned.
Chill 6 to 8 hours before serving. Serves 4.

Mme Jehane Benoit. *Enjoying the Art of Canadian Cooking.*
Toronto: Pagurian, 1974, p. 135.

CANADA'S APPLE STORY begins before the recorded history of North America, with two or three varieties of crabapple considered native here. How they first arrived on this continent is unclear; in fact, any specific information on the subject is guesswork at best. They were small, hard and green, not pleasant eating. John Laird Farrar, in *Trees in Canada*, writes that there are about twenty-five varieties of wild apple worldwide, of which two are native to Canada. One, *Malus coronaria* or *Pyrus coronaria*, is found only in southern Ontario. The other, *Malus fusca* or *Pyrus diversifolia*, the Pacific crabapple, grows along coastal British Columbia.

We know from early accounts that Native Canadians were able to make use of and enjoy this fruit. And, when apple trees from Europe were introduced, they were soon growing their own trees of the more succulent, imported fruit.

Our first record of native crabapples comes from Samuel de Champlain, who noted the raspberries and "little wild apples"

A visitor, describing his experiences on Vancouver Island in the 1860s, wrote:

"Crab-apples are wrapped in leaves and preserved in bags for winter. The method of cooking them, when fresh plucked, is by simply boiling the apples; but, when they have lost their acidity, they are cooked by being placed in a hole dug in the ground, over which green leaves are placed, and a fire kindled above all. The natives are as careful of their crab-apples as we are of our orchards; and it is a sure sign of their losing heart before intruding whites when, in the neighbourhood of settlements, they sullenly cut down their crab-apple trees, in order to gather the fruit for the last time without trouble, as the tree lies upon the ground."

Gilbert Malcolm Stoat. *Scenes and Studies of Savage Life*. London: Smith, Elder, 1868, p. 56.

he saw while exploring the region east of Georgian Bay in 1615.[6] In fact it was Champlain who, along with the settlers at Port Royal, first brought eating apples to North America.

No fruit was as important to North America's early settlers as the apple. Where settlements grew, apple orchards grew with them. All of these trees had to be brought to North America from Europe along with the settlers, either as saplings or as seeds, seeds that might result in apples no better than the wild crabs or, with luck, might develop into exciting new varieties.

The earliest recorded permanent settlers to the shores of what is now Canada were principally from Normandy. As might be expected, with them came apple cider. Throughout England, France and much of Europe the lakes and rivers were already polluted. Water, for the most part, was unsafe to drink and people had become dependent on wine, beer and cider. It isn't surprising then that for these early settlers the planting of an orchard, where the climate made it at all possible, was one of the first tasks to be undertaken as soon as enough land was cleared. Although some of these trees may have been seedlings brought from home, no doubt many were grown from seed and were of mixed quality, but all were good for cider.

Exactly where and when the first seeds or saplings arrived is still in question, but it is generally accepted that by 1610 the settlers at Port Royal (now Annapolis Royal) were growing apple trees from seed. Although this original settlement was later abandoned, cultivated apple trees were growing at LaHave, Acadia, by 1635. Nicholas Denys, Governor of Acadia at the time, wrote that year: "A missionary located in this territory had a beautiful garden in which were to be found several apple trees and pear trees all well rooted and in healthy condition."[7] In 1698 a French census

21

Although there is a portrait of Samuel de Champlain reproduced in many versions showing an elegant fellow with a lush moustache, it has long been known that this is not a true depiction of the man. The only authentic representation of Champlain is this engraving of a sketch originally done by Champlain himself included in his depiction of the battle on Lake Champlain in 1609.

The Champlain Society

recorded that there were 1584 apple trees growing on the property of the fifty-four Acadian families in Port Royal.

Champlain returned to New France in 1608 to establish a *habitation* further inland at Hochelaga (now Quebec City) where he found the land "beautiful and agreeable." In 1617 he brought more settlers from France, among them Louis Hébert and his wife, Marie Rollet, and their family. Champlain put Hébert, now immortalized as the first farmer of New France, in charge of the settlement gardens on the heights of Quebec City and, in particular, of the sapling apple trees he had brought from the highly successful orchards in Normandy. As early as 1623, Gabriel Sagard reported that a young apple tree from Normandy was bearing good fruit here. The little orchard didn't survive the occupation by the English following 1629, but the French later replanted and were producing a significant harvest by 1660; priests of the Sulpician order were tending the first significant orchard on the slopes of Mount Royal at about that time.

Some of the most detailed early records of eighteenth-century political and social life (including gardening and farming) in North America can be found in the writings of Pehr (or Peter) Kalm, a student of the great Swedish naturalist, Linnaeus. In 1748 the Swedish Academy of Sciences sent Kalm to North America to discover plants and trees suitable for the climate in Sweden. He travelled through New France and the northern area of what was to become the United States of America recording much of what he saw. In keeping with his mandate Kalm described the gardens he visited, and in Quebec City wrote: "The many great orchards and kitchen gardens near the house of the Jesuits and other public and private buildings make the town appear very large, though the number of houses it contains is not very great."[8] By

In the spring of 1624, Champlain reported: "the oak had its buds swelling, and the apples-trees we had transplanted from France, as well as the plum-trees, were budding ..."

The Works of Samuel de Champlain, vol. V: *Samuel de Champlain.* Toronto: Champlain Society, 1922–36, p. 122.

Jean Laframboise, in 1763, was one of the earliest settlers of Chazy on the west side of Lake Champlain. Now not far from the Quebec border, it was originally part of New France before it changed hands from French to British to Native and finally became part of the United States, where it has since remained. In spite of having his property burned out at least once, Laframboise persevered and became the first apple grower in the Lake Champlain area. Some of his original orchard acreage is now included in the famous Chazy Orchards in New York just south of the U.S. border.

this time it was said that, in Montreal, the Sulpicians were producing a hundred caskets of cider every year.

Apples were so important to the settlers that, even in areas where there are no commercial orchards today, they grew in individual orchards and provided essential foods for early households. They were eaten raw, of course. They were used in cooking in many ways – in pies and tarts, for apple sauce, apple vinegar, apple jelly and apple butter and, especially, for apple cider. They were also air-dried (often strung on lines over the kitchen stove or in the attic) and then stored, to provide a welcome addition to winter meals. Everywhere, their juice became the common beverage. Cider references appear frequently in early writings – how to make it, how to turn it into applejack, and (by early temperance advocates) how to resist it.

The earliest named Quebec apple was the Fameuse, sometimes called Pomme de Neige, and usually known in English

A French explorer and settler, Michel Guillaume Jean de Crèvecoeur, who lived in New York at the end of the eighteenth century (then still part of New France), described how apples were dried:

"Our method is this: we gather the best kind. The neighbouring women are invited to spend the evening at our house. A basket of apples is given to each of them, which they peel, quarter and core. These peelings and cores are put in another basket and when the intended quantity is thus done, tea, a good supper, and the best things we have are served up. The quantity I have thus peeled is commonly twenty baskets, which gives me about three of dried.

Next day a stage is erected either in our grass plots or anywhere else where cattle can't come. Strong crotches are planted in the ground ... poles fixed ... and a scaffold erected. The apples are thinly spread. They are soon covered with all the bees and wasps of the neighbourhood. This accelerates the operation of drying. Now and then they are turned. ... By this means we are enabled to have apple-pies and apple-dumplings almost the year around. ... My wife's and my supper half of the year consists of apple-pie and milk."[9]

Canada as a Snow. Its origin is unknown but it is believed to have first been grown near Montreal from a Normandy seedling. Whatever its source, it was grown as early as 1700 and, although it can be difficult to find these days, it is sought out by those who remember its crisp, juicy, white flesh sometimes threaded with red. Unfortunately, the Fameuse is subject to apple scab and, but for this one fault, wrote the author of *Fruits of Ontario* in 1914, "the Fameuse would be the most profitable [apple] of all, especially in Eastern Ontario, where it attains its highest perfection."[10] In 1874, Fameuse apples grown by farmers in Mont–Saint Hilaire, Quebec, won a gold medal in France for their excellent quality. These apples

Delos W. Beadle, one of the founders of the Fruit Growers' Association of Upper Canada, and a highly respected early horticulturalist, wrote of its value:

"Here it [the Fameuse] is grown in a perfection seldom elsewhere seen; here its fine qualities are fully brought out, and here its ruddy fruit is admired and appreciated by those of every age and every rank.

The tree is hardy, very hardy; standing in the next rank to the Siberian crabs, and thriving in any properly drained soil, in well-nigh every part of the Dominion. It is a moderate grower, with large glossy, green leaves and dark shoots, and bears abundantly and early. The fruit is dark red in the sun, growing lighter in the shade, where it is sometimes a pale greenish yellow; the flesh is snow white, very tender, breaking, juicy, almost melting, with a delicate aroma, and most agreeable mild flavour; quality, 'very good.'"

D.W. Beadle. *Canadian Fruit, Flower, and Kitchen Gardener*. Toronto: James Campbell, 1872, p. 70.

may be one of the ancestors of the more famous McIntosh, which would probably make it a very close relative because, unlike most apples, the Fameuse tends to breed true by seed.

By the last quarter of the nineteenth century, growers in the two major apple-growing regions of the province, near Quebec City and south and southeast of Montreal, were thriving and finding a ready market for their produce in Montreal and in other well-populated centres along the St. Lawrence.

THE CIDER MILLS OF MONTÉRÉGIE

Heading south from Quebec's major Highway 20, just east of Montreal, the traveller reaches one of the provinces most peaceful and beautiful apple regions, the Montérégie. The Montérégie contains 23 percent of Quebec's arable land, and this is the heart

Dwarf apple trees grown on trellises for easy picking and conservative use of the land at Cidrerie Michel Jodoin.

of the Quebec apple industry. Here the climate and the soil are particularly suited to apples; and centuries of experience and knowledge have contributed to the success of the orchards.

I headed that way on a sunny, Thanksgiving weekend, ready to taste the fruit and experience this scenic landscape at harvest time. The drive itself was particularly rewarding, taking me through a countryside quite different from that usually found in Quebec – fertile flat plains, *sere* fields of corn, rolling hills, all backed by the dense green of pine and cedar bush. It is an area full of attractive round rocks of a size that can be easily carried, and they can be seen everywhere – rock foundations, rock walls, piles of rocks, all abound. From Montreal south and east to the American border lies some of the best agricultural land in the province.

As I approached the American border, I was among the orchards. There were orchards everywhere, and everywhere, it seemed, were *les cidreries*, the cider mills.

I stopped at the Vergers Petch or Petch Orchards, a very busy place this fall weekend. Farmed by the third generation of the Petch family in Hemmingford, less than ten kilometres north of the American border, the orchards are family-friendly, a place where visitors are encouraged to pick their own apples, enjoy a picnic, take part in a tour, visit the on-site museum or enjoy the straw-bale maze. I bought some chilled, fresh apple juice and moved on.

This is one of the principal areas for the production of Quebec's famous ciders. The hard cider beverages produced here, and there are many varieties, are closer to wine than to what most of the rest of North America thinks of as cider, where it is equated with fresh or canned apple juice. I headed east across the peaceful Richelieu River to Rougemont, a region of numerous orchards and cider mills known as the apple capital of Quebec. Here, on the south slope of Rougemont Mountain, I found one of the province's major cider producers, winner of many awards for hard cider, sparkling cider and sparkling apple juice, Cidrerie Michel Jodoin. The surrounding orchard originated with one hundred apple trees bought by Michel Jodoin's grandfather in 1901. Now, all the apples harvested from the nine-hectare orchard are used in the cider mill – chiefly McIntosh, Lobo and Russet.

But Cidrerie Michel Jodoin is only one of the cider producers in the province. Among the many others are the award-winning Cidrerie du Minot in Hemmingford, which offers tours of

The tour at Cidrerie Michel Jodoin takes the visitor into a cellar devoted to the distilling and storage of cider that is itself a work of art. The doors, sculptures of apple trees complete with glistening red apples, lead to dark wood and brick walls forming an attractive background to the rows of white oak barrels in which juice is fermenting into a variety of ciders – rosé, aperitif, sparkling, champagne-style among them. The tour ends with a tasting that encourages the shopper to stock up on these special ciders.

Cidrerie Michel Jodoin

This nineteenth-century apple press is on view at Cidrerie du Minot, one of the earliest artisanal cider makers in Quebec. The press was brought to Canada from Brittany in about 1880 and belongs to the family of Robert Demoy. He and Joëlle Demoy are now owners of the mill, which benefits from a microclimate influenced by two rivers, the St. Lawrence and the Richelieu, as well as Lake Champlain to the south. This allows the Demoys to grow not only McIntosh, Cortland and Lobo, but also Geneva, Liberty, Trent and Golden Russet.
Cidrerie Minot

the estate that include their antique nineteenth-century family cider press, and Vinaigrerie Artisanale, which specializes in tonic vinegars. In Île-d'Orléans, farther north along the St. Lawrence near Quebec City, are Cidrerie Vergher Bilideau (featuring a maple syrup–flavoured cider) and Cidrerie du Domaine Steinbach (famous for its ducks, delicious meals and large range of cider products). There are cider mills at every turn throughout the apple-growing regions of Quebec. Most offer tours and entertainment as well as cider; the cider is also available in the province's liquor stores (*Société des alcools du Québec*).

In 1874 the Fameuse apple was awarded a gold medal in Lyon, France, which helped to establish Quebec's fame as a producer of superior cider. Cider's increasing popularity turned out to be a mixed benefit because it led to a struggle between the clergy (some of whom denounced the evils of drinking hard cider) and the cider producers. The producers rebelled and refused to pay their tithes to the church. But when Prohibition was adopted by the other provinces between 1915 and 1917, Quebec was the one holdout, passing a temperance Act instead, which allowed for the sale of cider as well as wine and beer.

An inventory of Quebec orchards in 1882 included the following varieties among the most favoured: Fameuse, Pomme Grise, Bourassa, Golden Russet, Tolman Sweet, Late Strawberry and Blue Permain.

THE GROWTH OF THE ORCHARDS

During the second half of the nineteenth century, the apple growers and educated amateurs who took a serious interest in agriculture pursued individual apple trials and shared their observations at meetings and informal organizations. "They were what we would call 'friends' of agriculture who made their own important contribution."[11]

Organizations such as the Agricultural and Horticultural Society of Montreal (1849), the Agricultural School of Ste-Anne-de-la-Pocatière (1859) and other horticultural societies in Abbotsford

Harvesting the apple crop at
Abbotsford, Quebec, in the 1890s

(1874) and Missisquoi (1879) left more formal records. (In 1876, the Montreal society sent 233 varieties of apples to the Philadelphia International Exposition!) Participants concentrated their efforts on developing varieties that could survive the sometimes bitterly cold winters of the region. At this time most of the orchards were on family farms and farmers were encouraged to grow as many as two or three dozen varieties. However, by the end of the century, diseases and insects were becoming difficult to control, and fewer varieties were advocated, with an emphasis on the Fameuse.

An important step in the scientific study of apple growing took place in 1890, when the Oka School of Agriculture was established at the Trappist Monastery west of Montreal. By that time "the Trappist orchards contained 2500 apple (150 varieties), 1500 plum, and 1500 cherry trees and a small vineyard. The nursery associated with the orchards had [already] shipped across the

Trappist monks on their way to
work, perhaps in the apple orchard,
circa 1900

Notman Photographic Archives,
McCord Museum of Canadian History,
Montreal MP-0000.27.138

Postulants and novices of the Sisters of Our Lady of the Holy Rosary of Rimouski, Quebec, in 1920 continue the work in the orchard that has been part of convent life since the seventeenth century.

Archives R.S.R.

country 100,000 trees grafted on European (French) rootstocks."[12] The school later became affiliated with the University of Montreal and in 1962 was replaced by the Faculty of Agriculture at Laval University in Quebec City.

As the century came to an end, in 1893 the province's three horticultural societies joined forces to become the Pomological and Fruit Growing Society of Quebec. This led to even more valuable exchanges of information. At the first meeting of the Society, members suggested that "science combined with practice" should be their motto. Concern about protecting the orchards from insects and disease had become a serious problem for the growers and was discussed at the meeting. John Craig and James Fletcher from the Experimental Farm in Ottawa (which had opened its doors in 1886) attended this first meeting and recommended that growers spray their trees "early and often with Bordeau mixture [four pounds bluestone and ten pounds of fresh lime in a barrel of water, with Paris green added to later sprayings]." Other advice was to wash the trunk of the trees with soap and water in the spring.

Professor Charles Gibb, founding member and a grower in Abbotsford, Quebec, became an important figure in the development of apple varieties appropriate to the Canadian climate. In 1882 he travelled to Russia and brought back Russian varieties, including Yellow Transparent, Duchess of Oldenburg and Russian Gravenstein, to be tested in Quebec and at the Experimental Farm in Ottawa. Of particular importance was his introduction of the exceptionally hardy *Malus baccata* which became important as a winter-hardy rootstock for many other varieties of apples and pears.

The twentieth century brought many changes to Quebec horticulture. Scientists and specialists took over from the knowledgeable amateurs and more formal training began to be available. William Macdonald, a Montreal philanthropist, cooperated with educators to bring practical agriculture to the schools. He funded the establishment of Macdonald College, which opened its doors in 1907 at Ste-Anne-de-Bellevue not far from Montreal. Later the college was affiliated with McGill University. William Saxby Blair, who went on to the Experimental Fruit Station at Kentville in Nova Scotia, was hired as the first horticulturalist at the college. Dr. James Robertson, first principal of Macdonald

"I remember how the marketwomen of Paris, wheeling barrows of apples of doubtful origin, used to cry them as 'Canada! Des vraies Canada!'"

Quoted in *Colombo's Canadian Quotations*. John Robert Colombo. Edmonton: Hurtig, 1974, p. 432; from *The European Discovery of America: The Northern Voyages AD 500–1600*, 1971.

College, was responsible for the earliest cold storage shipments of fruit (including apples) to the United Kingdom.

As part of the work of the horticultural department at Macdonald College, twenty-five acres (about ten hectares) were set aside for an orchard. The killing frosts of the winters of 1917–18 and 1933–34 made it clear to the department that developing hardier stock more suited to the Quebec conditions would be their major task. After the severe frosts, most of the earlier trees had to be replaced. "All replacements have been made with one object in view," wrote the college historian in 1963, "to have better varieties and hardier trees for the Quebec orchards."[13]

By 1927 it had become apparent that the enormous market for apples in Quebec was being increasingly replaced by imports from other provinces, in part because the Quebec growers were producing a wide variety of apples, many of which had little appeal in the market. In a move to change this, members of the Pomological

The apple stall at Bonsecours Market, Montreal, Quebec

Canadian Illustrated News, 1880 (1970.228). Stewart Museum, Montreal (Canada)

Society opened a new apple–growing area just north of the Vermont border, centred at Frelighsburg. Here they planted more popular apples – McIntosh, Fameuse, Melba, Lobo and later Cortland. For added winter protection the rootstock *Malus robusta 5*, developed by P. Omer Roy at St–Jean–sur–Richelieu Research Station of Ottawa's Experimental Farm, began to be used widely.

Today, the objectives of Quebec's apple–breeding program continue to be "to develop hardy and disease resistant varieties for the production of juice and cider and/or varieties with an

Photograph by Malak

excellent fruit quality and a long shelf life."[14] Recent cultivars released by the research station at St-Jean-sur-Richelieu and developed or tested at its substation in Frelighsburg are Belmac, Galarina, Primevere, Reinette Russet (a variety from France recommended for cider as a replacement for Golden Russet), Richelieu and Rouville. For the home gardener it recommends the new MacExel.

About half the apples now grown in Quebec are for the fresh market, to be either stored and sold through packers or (to a lesser extent) made available locally in stores, farmers' markets, roadside stands or pick–your–own orchards. The rest are processed, mainly for juice or cider, although some end up as sauce, frozen slices or pie fillings. Very few are exported.[15] The principal apples grown are Lodi (Early Golden), Vista Belle, Melba, Jersey Mac, Paulared, Lobo, McIntosh, Spartan, Cortland, Empire, Golden Russet and Delicious.

3

INTO THE MARITIMES

Apple Pandowdy

Slice five or six apples into a deep dish. Add 3 tbsp sugar, 4 tbsp molasses, nutmeg, cinnamon, and salt to taste and mix together. Cover and bake in a moderate (350°F) oven until soft, then cover with a rich baking powder biscuit crust, extending over the sides and bake for 15–20 minutes longer. Serve by cutting the crust into the apple and smothering with cream.

Julie V. Watson. *Favourite Recipes from Old Prince Edward Island Kitchens.* Halifax: Nimbus, 1996, p. 202.

FOLLOWING THE SAINT JOHN RIVER

After leaving the beautiful and productive Montérégie, I headed northeast and followed the south shore of the St. Lawrence River. The hills in the distance were glowing in every shade of the colours of fall, made even more dramatic by the deep green of the surrounding evergreens. The river widens into the Gulf at Rivière-du-Loup. From there I followed New Brunswick's Highway #2 as it traced swooping curves along the Saint John River valley towards the province's apple country. I seemed to be travelling through a beautiful, empty landscape. It was the middle of October and here too the trees were in full autumn colour. They hid the towns and villages that I knew existed below. As I arrived at the motel in Grand Falls where I planned to spend the night, I hoped for the memorable view the name suggests, but the dam hides all but the most obvious signs of what must have once been an amazing waterfall.

The next morning I headed for Corn Hill Nursery. I have been aware of Bob Osborne's nursery for some years and, in fact, last year bought a first generation McIntosh sapling from Corn Hill by mail. I wanted to visit the nursery in person and hear how Bob's interest in heritage apples had developed. Located in zone 4b about thirteen kilometres from Petitcodiac, the nursery grows and sells fruit trees and ornamental shrubs as well as herbaceous perennials. Bob Osborne grew up in Connecticut in the United States but came to New Brunswick with his parents about thirty years ago. Here they discovered that the shallow, fertile soil of the gently rolling hills of Kings County was ideal for the nursery they planned to create. The retail store and Cedar Café at the nursery are a tribute to the trees of the region and the architectural heritage of

Honeycrisp, the apple considered by the Kentville Station to be an important part of the future of apple production in the Atlantic Provinces.

S. Khanizadeh, "Our Apples," www.cyberfruit.info

the Maritime barn, both much admired by Bob Osborne. Working on the building using a wide variety of "these wonderful plants" including cedar, red oak, curly pear, maple, hemlock, birch and apple, was a labour of love for Osborne.

The nursery specializes in hardy apple trees, although the high cost of shipping has recently become a problem. In addition to McIntosh, such heritage varieties as Duchess of Oldenburg, Wealthy and Wolf River are available, as well as the more recent Novamac, Paulared, Spartan, Cortland and the newest favourite, Honeycrisp.

THE FIRST ORCHARDS

The earliest settlers in New Brunswick (at that time Acadia), were the French, some of whom came from Nova Scotia after they were deported from Grand Pré in 1755. They, like the rest of the

Young Honeycrisp trees at Corn Hill Nursery. It takes five years to bring these into production.

settlers in Atlantic Canada, would already have been growing apples for their own use. But apple production increased significantly with the arrival of the United Empire Loyalists in 1783 after the American Revolution. The Loyalists brought with them apple seedlings or seeds from their well-established orchards in New England. One of the earliest apple successes was a tree that grew from a seed planted by Lieutenant James Eccles, a Loyalist who had served in the King's New Brunswick Regiment and settled in Fredericton in the early part of the nineteenth century. The Eccles apple, as it became known, was a large, green apple excellent for cooking and storing. It was propagated for over a century and it is said that one of these trees still survives. The settlers' small holdings spread north along the Saint John River and this remains the main apple-growing region of the province today.

With the increase in population resulting from the influx of Loyalists, New Brunswick became a separate province in 1784.

"When [the Acadians] were deported, they left behind the cultivated fields, the fertile dykelands, and, of course, the apple trees. All over the province from Annapolis to Windsor and elsewhere, small orchards beside the ruins of French homes went on bearing fruit as though nothing had happened."

Anne Hutten. *Valley Gold: The Story of the Apple Industry in Nova Scotia.* Halifax: Petheric, 1981, p. 3.

Commercial production of apples in New Brunswick had to wait for the genius of Francis Peabody Sharp, the man known as the Father of Fruit Culture in the province. Sharp began experimenting with developing new varieties of fruit trees and grapes in 1846, when he was only twenty-three years old. Three years

Francis Peabody Sharp, "Father of Fruit Culture" in New Brunswick

New Brunswick Museum, Saint John, NB, Edwin Tappan Adney and Francis Peabody Sharp fonds F6

later he was operating the first commercial nursery in the province where he introduced high-density planting and the dwarfing of trees. At that time he and Peter Gideon of Minnesota were the only scientific hybridizers in all of North America.

Like all successful growers, Sharp recognized that the development of a successful nursery and orchard must take into account the climatic conditions of the region. Some of the varieties of apples he produced, such as Crimson Beauty, continued to be popular long after his death in 1903. The most popular of all was the New Brunswick apple, a close relative of, and sometimes confused with, the Duchess of Oldenburg. Every homestead of the day had a New Brunswick tree in the orchard.

Thanks to the skill and enthusiasm of Sharp, by the end of the nineteenth century New Brunswick had a commercial apple industry. Until 1911 many varieties of apples were still being grown; then a move towards monoculture changed the industry significantly. Earlier varieties that were difficult to ship or didn't have immediate eye appeal were discouraged, with the result that many well-loved apples that families remembered for their special, unique qualities began to disappear.

By 1903 a fruit growers' association had been formed and production increased over the decades until 1969, when international competition began to cut into the export trade of the province. In 1970 a number of small growers, regretting the loss of valuable early varieties, set out to rescue as many as possible. They had help and encouragement from the North America Fruit Explorers and other organizations interested in heritage varieties. Now popular early apples, such as Wealthy and Yellow Transparent, can still be found at roadside stands in New Brunswick.

INTO THE ANNAPOLIS VALLEY

Nova Scotia's Annapolis Valley must surely be one of the best apple-growing regions in the world. From the Minas Basin in the east to Annapolis Royal in the west (the home of the first apple trees brought to North America by Samuel de Champlain in 1604), the red loamy soil, the friendly climate of warm fall days and cool nights, and the protected valley all combine to make it the perfect home for fruit.

I entered Nova Scotia's apple paradise at Kentville, home of the Atlantic Food and Horticultural Research Centre. Here we are in the land of Evangeline and close to Grand Pré, site of a monument to the thousands of Acadians deported from there by the English between 1755 and 1763. I had come with an introduction to Charles Embree, Research Scientist there. Charlie, as he seems to be known to all, didn't know I was coming but immediately welcomed me and introduced me to the apple people and places I should see.

The Centre was created in 1910 as an Experimental Fruit Station, under the famous Dominion Horticulturalist, W.T. Macoun. An enthusiastic and energetic collector, Macoun discovered and named sixty-nine flowering plants, mosses and lichens. His seven-part *Catalogue of Canadian Plants* won him respect in Canada and abroad. The Macoun apple is named in his honour. The Centre's original 250 acres, part of a land grant to the United Empire Loyalists, was gradually added to until it now covers 463 acres plus a nearby farm, allowing plenty of room for research projects.

My first stop was the Blair House Museum, a charming old frame house with the wide verandah of an earlier day, now a museum devoted to the apple industry. Established by the Nova

"There is, perhaps, no country in the world, the States of American Union not excepted, better fitted for the growth of apples and pears than three or four of the Western [Nova Scotia] counties. We believe there is scarcely a County in the Province that is not capable of producing good apples and pears, if they receive ordinary attention in propagating and fertilizing; but in the Counties referred to, namely, Hants, Kings, Annapolis and Digby, the fruit is unsurpassed ..."

Dr. Alexander Forrester of the NSFGA, writing in 1883. Quoted in Norman H. Morse, "An Economic History of the Apple Industry of the Annapolis Valley in Nova Scotia" unpublished thesis, 1952.

Scotia Fruit Growers' Association (NSFGA), it is situated on the grounds of the Research Station and is named after the station's first superintendent, Dr. William Saxby Blair. One room of the museum is devoted to the history of the apple industry in the province with apple barrels, apple peelers and other artefacts, as well as many period photographs. In other rooms the history of the scientific research undertaken by the station right up to the present is outlined, with exhibits of the equipment used and pictures of science at work.

A PERFECT CLIMATE

Charlie Embree and I later drove to the top of the North Mountain from which there was a wonderful view of the valley below. The mountain is actually a high ridge rising 650 feet (200 metres) above the waters of the Bay of Fundy, protecting the Annapolis Valley from that direction, while the gentle slope of the South Mountains cups the valley, creating a unique microclimate that seems perfectly designed for fruit growing. Some of the richest soil of the area is deep silt created by the flood plains of the Minas Basin, once it had been cleared of salt and protected from incoming tides by the ingenious dykes and draining aboiteaux (sluice gates) built by early Acadians.

Early settlers here grew a mix of apple trees for their own use, usually from scions (grafting branches) brought from Normandy as early as 1604, or as pippins that sprang naturally from planted or discarded seeds. The apples were not always dependable for good eating, but the mix made a palatable cider – of major importance in these early households.

The cultivation of apples began to become more sophisticated in 1812, when Charles R. Prescott, a successful businessman

"Every fall father put a barrel of Northern Spys and a barrel of Winter Gravensteins and a box of Russets in the basement. Apples were accepted as if they went naturally with a house and land in much the same way as old lilacs and roses."

Beatrice Ross Buszek.
Apple Connection: Cookery with Flavour, Fact and Folklore...
Halifax: Nimbus, 1985, p. xii.

48

"Apple peeling frolics were part of the social life, with entire families and their neighbours sitting around a farmhouse kitchen paring and cutting the fruit, stringing them on cotton twine by means of a darning needle."

Anne Hutten. *Valley Gold: The Story of the Apple Industry in Nova Scotia*. Halifax: Petheric, 1981, p. 46.

Mary Evans Picture Library, 10043669

from Halifax, moved to the Annapolis Valley. He had already made his fortune by the time he was forty and was looking for a healthier climate. The Annapolis Valley, with fifty-five more days of sunshine than most of the rest of Nova Scotia, beckoned. At Starr's Point on the Minas Basin across the Cornwallis River from Wolfville, Prescott built a beautiful Georgian house where he lived until his death in 1859.

Once settled at Starr's Point, Prescott was able to indulge his passion for horticulture. At a time before Nova Scotia had any commercial growers, and when fruits, vegetables and ornamental plants were bred to be grown in the warmer climates of Europe or the American eastern seaboard, he began to seek out and introduce plants more suited to Nova Scotia. It was no easy task! Locating, ordering and shipping plant materials was a time-consuming, logistical challenge. Just arranging for plants to be safely delivered to this out-of-the-way corner of the world was a risky business. In spite of this, Prescott was soon growing fruits of all kinds in his greenhouse. His greatest successes, however, were in his extensive orchard. He tested and introduced an astonishing number of varieties – over a hundred. From these he concentrated on twenty-seven of the best for his permanent orchard. As he experimented, he invited local farmers to come into his orchard and learn how to graft trees, sending them home with buds and scions to begin their own orchards. It is not surprising to hear that he was one of the founders of the Nova Scotia Fruit Growers' Association. His most important introduction was the Gravenstein, which became one of the mainstays of Nova Scotia's apple industry over the next century and a half.

Orchards in Nova Scotia are all still family-owned, many by those who have been here for generations, even for centuries.

Acacia Grove, the house built by Charles Prescott on the Cornwallis River, as it is today. After his death in 1859, the house fell into serious disrepair. The fine furniture was sold; the Acacia trees for which it was named were cut down; at one time itinerant labourers used it as a hostel as they passed through the area; and eventually livestock was housed on the ground floor. The house would probably have been torn down but for a happy coincidence in 1930. Prescott's great-granddaughter, Mary Allison Prescott, while on vacation in the area from her home in Montreal, saw the house and was determined to restore it. She had massive repairs undertaken, purchased furniture from her great-grandfather's period, and even recovered many of the old family photos. She and her two spinster sisters lived there until her death in 1969. The house was left to the province with the request that it become an historic site and so it remains to this day, open to visitors for six months of the year.

Nova Scotia Museum,
History Collection, Halifax

51

Gravenstein apple winners, Kentville

Although Charles Prescott is believed to have grafted and tested more than a hundred apple varieties, he is remembered chiefly for the following thirteen: Ribston, Blenheim, King of Pippins, Gravenstein, Alexander and Golden Pippin from England; Baldwin, Rhode Island Greening, Sweet Bough and Northern Spy from the United States; Fameuse, Pomme Grise and Canada Reinette from Montreal. The most important apples of these were Northern Spy and Gravenstein (a seventeenth-century apple originating in Germany). Both have remained important commercial crops for Nova Scotia's apple industry. The Northern Spy, a late-maturing apple, keeps well and is especially good for cooking. The Gravenstein, an aromatic, flavourful fruit, is equally good for eating, cooking or processing. It can be grown commercially in very few places – in North America only in Sonoma County, California and the Annapolis Valley. The Gravenstein is considered by many to be the best apple in the world for pies.

Several of these families, including the Spurrs and the Aylwards, continue to provide the market with some of the best apples in Canada.

The Elderkins, for example, received a land grant in 1760. They found deserted orchards still thriving then, and have been growing apples in Kentville ever since. I met with Paul Elderkin. Still an active grower, he remembers when local independent stores bought directly from the growers and there were many wholesalers in Halifax providing a market for the rest of the crop. Now Sobeys and Loblaws control the retail market. Sarsfield Foods, the Kentville pie plant now owned by Weston's, is an almost insatiable market producing an incredible one hundred thousand pies a day!

By the late 1850s, farmers were beginning to realize that there was money to be made in growing apples. Halifax was becoming a significant market and with the completion of the Nova Scotia railway in 1858, apples could reach that market the same day they were picked. From there, apples were shipped by sail to Liverpool in England and Boston in the United States.

A major breakthrough came in 1860 and 1862. The best apples exhibited in Halifax were shipped to London for the Royal Horticultural Society's International Fruit and Vegetable Show. Here they were awarded a silver medal and seven bronze medals.

One of the 10 million apple pies turned out each year at Sarsfield Foods in Kentville. An important market for the growers in Nova Scotia, they buy about 15 million pounds of Northern Spys each year which they peel, core and slice as required throughout the twelve months.
Sarsfield Foods Ltd.

Apples are still picked by hand today. Pickers use baskets, which they empty into bins. The Nova Scotia apples website gives detailed instructions on apple picking. A good worker can fill four bins in a day, each holding about 2250 apples!

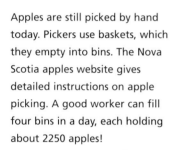

"This Nova Scotia collection is in itself worth a visit to the exhibition," wrote the *London Times*. "It is small but it beats anything we have ever seen." The superiority of Nova Scotia apples was immediately established. Britain became the province's main market for apples, which were shipped principally to London where they were allowed free entry. Keeping the fruit fresh was always a problem: one way to control the temperature in early times was to cover the shipments with ice-coated lumber.

As New England orchards began producing enough apples for their own use, they imposed a duty on imported apples, so Nova Scotia growers concentrated on shipping apples overseas and, in 1885, Annapolis County alone shipped ninety thousand barrels to London and Liverpool. Apples had become the major crop of the county. About two hundred varieties were grown,

54

"One of the sights of this valley is the orchard of Mr. W.C. Archibald, of Wolfville. It contains some 500 apple trees and about 4000 plum trees, all laden with fruit. These trees are set so closely that, when bowed down, as they are this summer, with their burden of fruit, a walk through the orchard involves a great deal of stooping and tortuous meandering. The trees stand as a rule about seven feet apart and their branches are completely entwined. All are well laden, Mr. Archibald being now engaged in gathering a crop of at least 500 barrels apples and 2,000 bushels plums."

The Berwick Register, September 1899

Packing apples at Middleton, N.S. Although apples had long been shipped in barrels, the market began to complain that they did not offer enough protection, and by the early twentieth century boxes were gaining favour.

Nova Scotia Museum, History Collection, Halifax 40909

but over the following decade or two, the most popular tended to be Gravenstein (especially a red sport), Ribston, Nonpareil, Golden Russet, King, Spy and Baldwin. Trees bought from New England tree peddlers soon proved to be unsatisfactory and, before long, local nurseries began to develop.

Barrels of Nova Scotia apples ready
for shipping to Britain, circa 1922

Notman Photographic Archives,
McCord Museum of Canadian History,
Montreal MP-0000.25.478

As production increased early in the twentieth century, insects and diseases, such as black spot, began to be a problem, and spraying, which had been introduced in the 1880s, became more common. By now growers had organized as the Nova Scotia Fruit Growers' Association (NSFGA) and were petitioning the government for research help. In 1912 the federal government responded by opening the experimental station at Kentville. Frost was another major problem if the apples were to be stored prior to shipping, so frost-proof warehouses were built along the rail lines and on the docks in Halifax. But protecting apples during shipping remained difficult and British buyers had to be compensated for those that arrived in severely damaged condition. The fault lay with the growers as often as with the shippers, and grading and inspecting of shipments was a constant task. Not enough care was being taken to pack good clean apples securely. The wisdom of shipping in barrels was questioned too. Boxes, smaller than barrels, gave apples better protection. Australia was shipping in boxes and could demand higher prices on the London market. But shipping in barrels meant that Nova Scotia growers could offer more apples at a lower price, even though this meant they concentrated on cooking apples rather than dessert apples.

All in all, competition from Ontario and the rest of the world was increasing and by the first two decades of the twentieth century apples from Ontario and the United States were competing for the London market, while Nova Scotia was now selling mainly to Liverpool and northern England. Every region was affected by the weather and this meant that sometimes one region, sometimes another, had superior apples – something that continues to be true in all orchards to this day. Meanwhile, the

Scotian Gold Co-operative Limited, established in 1957, grew from the roots of the United Fruit Companies of Nova Scotia of 1912. It is owned by the producers themselves and distributes more than 25 percent of the province's apple crop fruit from about fifty growers.

Scotian Gold Co-operative Limited

industry in British Columbia was growing and beginning to threaten that of Nova Scotia. All these factors, including the planning and promoting of exhibitions, and the question of how much cooperative selling should be undertaken, provided the NSFGA with problems that were discussed endlessly over the years. Finally, the United Fruit Companies of Nova Scotia Limited was organized in 1912 to carry on marketing activities for a number of the growers. Others asserted their independence by relying on individual shippers.

By the 1930s, production in England was increasing; because the Nova Scotia orchards were ageing, a major effort was made to renew them with new trees and new grafts on older rootstocks. One result of the Depression years was the establishment of the Ottawa Agreements with Britain that gave apples from the Empire a preference in the United Kingdom. Exports from the United States declined, and, for a time, Nova Scotia became the largest supplier of apples to Britain. In 1933 the province recorded its largest crop ever with an estimated 8.3 million bushels, most of which were exported to England. But four years later, when the preference was reduced, Nova Scotia turned its eyes back to the home market.

With the outbreak of war in 1939, restrictions were placed on apple exports and the *War Measures Act* that year centralized sales. As exports were cut, growers suffered losses in spite of the relief offered by government programs. Increases in the processing of apples took up some of the slack. By 1945 these included dried and canned apples, juice, concentrates and pie filling.

After the war, with the continued decline of sales to Britain, stress was put on improving the industry. Apples were to be packed in boxes rather than barrels, small acreages were discouraged, improved cold storage extended the season, new grafts of the most popular varieties were made – Gravenstein, McIntosh, Cortland, Red Delicious, Spy and Rome Beauty.

Thanks to the provincial entomologist A.D. Pickett, a major change in the control of apple pests was undertaken in Nova Scotia about this time. He saw that the indiscriminate use of sprays, which destroyed the useful insects along with the harmful, was doing more harm than good and advocated a more controlled use. At first his views were given no official support and he had to fight for them; his instructions from Ottawa were: "con-

Dr. A.D. Pickett was instrumental in convincing growers across the country to take environmental effects into account when using pest controls in the orchard.

Agriculture and Agri-Food Canada, Kentville, NS

tinue to test pesticides, forget about ecological studies, and don't concern yourself about long-term effects on the environment."[16] But the Nova Scotia growers were paying attention to Pickett and the new program was working. By the end of the decade the rest

"Every year the festival had a different theme. For 1935 someone envisioned hundreds of multicoloured Maypole dances, a seemingly chaste and decorous rite to honour the miracle of the blossoms. On the fated day, hundreds of school children skipped and tripped onto the field to the shrill notes of the swirling skirted pipers. And then, having practiced to perfection, we picked up the long ribbons and wove them in and out and under to make a perfect Maypole.

"As the train approached Grand Pré and Wolfville, there were miles of orchards as far as the eye could see, bedecked in deep pink buds about to bloom. The early June air, though cool, was saturated with the heady pervasive bouquet of apple orchards in the spring."

Beatrice Ross Buszek, arriving for the Apple Blossom Festival as a schoolgirl in 1935. *Apple Connection: Cookery with Flavour, Fact and Folklore ...* Halifax: Nimbus, 1985, pp. xi-xii.

Nova Scotia Museum, History Collection, Halifax 40134

Nova Scotia
Apple Production, 1989 & 1999,
by thousands of bushels

	1989	1999
McIntosh	950	1000
Cortland	300	324
Spy	270	226
Gravenstein	200	160
Delicious	220	160

"We commenced using our potatoes Aug. 4th and have enough for a month yet. We sold $15. Worth of currants and our little girls got $11. For strawberries and raspberries. I have sold $24. Worth of apples and have 13 barrels of winter keeping apples on hand. I got $1.00 a bus. Or $3.00 a barrel."

Personal letter, John T. Weeks, Alberton, PEI, to his brother, November 6, 1903

of the country began to follow suit; spraying was reduced and natural predators were encouraged. Now most growers follow the Integrated Pest Management system (IPM), monitoring the orchards and making use of natural predators and parasites, along with a minimum of pesticides. The whole operation is thus more environment–friendly.

Although the overall crop has declined since the high in 1933, apples still dominate life in the Annapolis Valley today – apples for export around the world, fresh apples for the local market on the many roadside stands, and an amazing 60+ per-cent of the crop for processing. The Apple Blossom Festival is cel-ebrated up and down the valley with pancake breakfasts, dessert contests, craft fairs, art shows, carnivals, musical concerts, parades and fireworks.

Perfect conditions in 2002 meant that the apple harvest was the best in years – resulting in a heavy crop of beautiful, large fruit and a 31.7 percent increase over the previous year. For the first time in many years, buyers from Ontario and Quebec were supplementing their less successful harvests with apples from the Valley.

OVER ON THE ISLAND

A small orchard was as much a part of pioneer life in Prince Edward Island as it was throughout much of North America, even though the climate is more challenging here than in the major apple–producing regions, and early growers were able to take top prizes in fruit exhibitions in Paris and Glasgow in 1900 and 1901. There are believed to have been close to two thousand hectares of orchards in the province at the turn of the twentieth century, and they were essential to the small farmer in those early years.

A decade or two later, however, apple production in the province began a decline that continued until recent years. Disease, in particular apple scab, and pests such as codling moths and maggots, took their toll. It was soon difficult to compete with orchards in Nova Scotia's warmer climate, and the increasing competition from foreign producers.

In the past decade or two, however, new developments in commercial trees have seen improvements for PEI growers. Dwarf and semi-dwarf trees, better suited to the island climate, have become available and, although the export market remains negligible, apple growers are hopeful of beginning to replace imports with more locally grown varieties such as McIntosh, Cortland, Spartan and Paulared. In 1999, the PEI Department of Agriculture and Forestry reported: "The acreage of apple orchards in PEI has doubled over the last six years." They foresaw the same increase over the coming three years. Marketing is chiefly through U-Pick operations, although making cider and other apple products is carried out on a small scale. An integrated fruit production plan was outlined in 2000 with the objective of improving horticultural practices in the province. Ö

"The apple Blossoms were out and the world was fresh and young."

Lucy Maud Montgomery. *Anne of Green Gables*. Boston: 1908. Reprint, Toronto: Everyman's Library Children's Classics, 1995, p. 371.

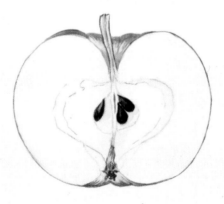

EDGAR.   McINTOSH X FOREST

4
ONTARIO'S WONDERFUL DISCOVERY

Apple Butter or Apple Sauce

This is often made in the houses of settlers where there is an abundance of apples, on a large scale; several bushels of pared apples being boiled down, either in cider or with water, for several hours, til the whole mass is throughly incorporated. Great care is needful to keep it stirred, so as to prevent burning. There are several ways of making this apple–butter: some make it with cider, others without, some use sugar, others do not; some boil sliced pumpkin with the apples if the latter are very acid. It is a standing dish in most American houses, and is very convenient.

Catharine Parr Traill. *The Canadian Settler's Guide.* Toronto: 1855. Reprint, New Canadian Library. Toronto: McClelland & Stewart, 1969, p. 67.

Facing Page, McIntosh, one of the beautiful apple illustrations by Central Experimental Farm botanical artist Faith Files

THE COUNTY

I LIVE IN ONTARIO, half an hour north of Belleville where, just off-shore, Prince Edward County – the County, as it is referred to locally – is a long finger, almost an island, that points out into Lake Ontario. Its unusual position gives it a warmer (and in winter, stormier) climate than the mainland. In the past it was a major supplier of food for much of early Canada and was known, in particular, for its tomato and vegetable canneries – and its beautiful and productive orchards.

One sunny spring day in 2001, I drove to Picton, the major town in the County. I had often visited the area since making my home nearby, but this time I was looking for more specific information on the apple growers and their history.

Macaulay Heritage Park is an excellent place to begin a search for the history of Prince Edward County. The park, which includes a house, a museum in what was once St. Mary Magdalene Church, and a cemetery, is based on the original property of the Macaulay family. Reverend William Macaulay, son of the original Loyalist settler, Captain Robert Macaulay, was given a grant of five hundred acres in 1803. Here he gradually built the church and house that still survive on the property; and here, around the inlet now called Adolphus Reach, the town of Picton grew until it surrounded Macaulay Park. The family home, allowed to deteriorate for many years, has now been restored to its 1853 elegance. It was the small orchard on the grounds that I found particularly interesting.

As part of the restoration of the house and grounds to what they would have been like in the 1850s, a local pomologist, Henry Gray, was asked to recreate an orchard of the period. With the help of two original letters sent by John Macaulay in the 1850s ordering

Waupoos is an extraordinarily beautiful area of the County, moderated by Lake Ontario breezes and well suited to the growing of fruit, in particular apples and grapes. The County Cider Company, an estate winery specializing in hard ciders, is located here. The farm has been producing apples for more than 150 years and includes an historic stone farmhouse, built in 1835; a cidery in what was originally a cold storage building; the Tasting Room housed in an old stone barn; an outdoor café with a spectacular view of the lake and the surrounding countryside; and the orchard consisting of fifteen acres of Ida Red, Northern Spy, Golden Russets, McIntosh, Cortland and Red Delicious trees.

Photograph by Peggy deWitt, Picton

Few modern orchards are without
a beehive or two nearby. Bees are
essential to the successful fertilization
of the apple blossoms.

Photograph by Bev Wigney,
http://magickcanoe.com

apple trees and other plants, Gray set to work. (One of the letters was to a famous Canadian horticulturalist of the day, Chauncey Beadle, educated at the Ontario Agricultural College but best known for his work with azaleas in the southern United States.)

Finding these heritage trees in 1980 when Gray began was a serious challenge, but he took it up with enthusiasm. Henry Gray had his own "Hobby Orchard," as his sign proclaimed, just outside Picton. He had retired to this area about forty years previously, and had gradually built up an astonishing heritage orchard of more than 160 varieties. Many of the trees had grafts of multiple varieties, and he told amusing stories about how he had acquired them, including one about how he hid them in his pant leg while crossing the border from the United States! Among his favourites in the orchard were Strawberry Pippin, Cox's Orange Pippin and St. Lawrence.

While wandering around Macaulay Park, I had the good fortune to meet Philip Kennedy of Arbour Gardens, the volunteer groundsman. He told me the story of the orchard, showed me some of the related archives and suggested that I go to see Mr. Gray, who turned out to be a delightful raconteur, happy to talk about his forty years of "retirement." He was particularly proud of two apples in the orchard: the Lady apple, a variety believed to be about five thousand years old and described in the 1914 *Fruits of Ontario* as "a beautiful little apple for the amateur's collection";[17] and Seek-no-further, "an old commercial variety, at one time considerably planted in some parts of Ontario, and still highly valued by some apple growers."[18]

On subsequent trips, I continued my search through the County on the lookout for interesting orchards. They seemed to be everywhere. The many orchards here continue to be cultivated, as

The following apple trees were ordered by John Macaulay in 1852 and 1853 for the Macaulay orchard in Prince Edward County: Hubbardston Non-such, American Gold Russet, Canada Russet, Lacquier, Ladies Sweeting, Dyer or Pomme Royal, Newton Pippin, Newton Pippin Yellow, Rambo, Tolman Sweet, Benoni, Gravenstein, Swayze Pomenefrise [Pomme Grise], Rosburghii Russet, English Gold Pippin and Northern Spy.

they began, on family farms. The names of some of those early settlers can still be seen on the orchard signs along many of the country roads – Hughes, Doorn, Onderdonk. In the beautiful Waupoos area, southeast of Picton, the more recent vineyards have begun to compete for room with the orchards. Suddenly I felt that I had been magically transported to some more southern clime where lush green fields stretched to the brilliant blue of the

Campbell's Orchards & Country Market

Photograph by Jeremy Martin

lake, and in the ditches of the narrow, winding road, hollyhocks of every imaginable colour bloomed.

Later, as I drove to the other end of the county, I found Campbell's Orchards & Country Market. Like so many of today's orchard growers, Colin and Dianne Campbell have expanded sales by maintaining a store on the property and developing enter–tainment that draws visitors to the site to pick their own apples in September and October, or to buy the sweet apple cider pro–

The Big Apple is a favourite stopping place for travellers on Highway 401. The apple pies and other pastry treats are justly famous.
Photograph by Jeremy Martin

duced on the premises. In addition to apples and other fruit and vegetables, the store is full of unusual items – pastries, jams and gifts of all kinds. Special events are held at the orchard at Easter and Thanksgiving, and at Christmas mulled cider is served and mulling spice balls are available to take home.

EARLY DAYS

Pioneer orchards sprang up in the province all along Lake Ontario and the St. Lawrence River. From the beginning this was one of the most important apple-producing areas in the country. And here many of the important early varieties were discovered and flourished: Canada Red, St. Lawrence, Ontario, Scarlet Pippin, and, most notable of all, McIntosh.

Highway 2, running west from Belleville and Prince Edward County, is part of the Apple Route centred on Brighton. In September, Brighton's Applefest attracts crowds of visitors to its

71

fruit stands and markets, tearooms and cafés, museums and baking contests. And, of course, everyone goes home with baskets full of luscious apples fresh from the orchards. The apple displays are more inventive every year.

The United Empire Loyalists first began to settle in this area in 1783 and it soon became known that, situated on the shore of Lake Ontario as it is, it was an ideal location for growing fruit of all kinds.

One of these early settlers was Samuel Strickland, brother of the writers Catharine Parr Traill and Susanna Moodie. He wrote in

The house of apples, one of the elaborate early-twentieth-century displays at the Royal Winter Fair in Toronto

Elizabeth Chatten

"Canada can boast of as fine orchards as can be found in any part of the world. From the river Trent to Belleville on the Bay of Quinte, for twelve miles the road runs between almost a continuous line of them. In the month of May, when the trees are in full blossom, nothing can exceed the beauty of the country. That lovely sheet of water, the Bay of Quinte, runs parallel to this pretty chain of orchards, the ground sloping gently towards the shore, fringed here and there with groves of hickory and butternut, which tend greatly to increase the natural beauty of the scene."

Samuel Strickland. *Twenty-seven Years in Canada West, or, The Experience of an Early Settler.* London: Bentley, 1853, pp. 151–2.

Photograph by Peggy deWitt, Picton

"One of the first things I did after I moved into my new house was to sow a bed in the garden with apple-pips. This was in 1833, and as soon as the young stocks were large enough, I grafted them with the choicest fruit I could obtain – about one hundred – which I planted out the following year in an orchard to the south of my house. A year or two afterwards, I planted a hundred and fifty trees in a second orchard, north of the house, besides a great variety of plums and greengages. The last apple trees I set out were seedlings: I waited until they bore fruit, and then selected those trees I disapproved of, for grafting. By these means I have now two capital orchards, which last year gave me upwards of a hundred bushels of as fine fruit as can be produced in the country, amongst which may be enumerated the Ribstone pippin, Newtown pippin, Pearmain, Pomme-de-gris, Pomme-de-neige and many other sorts equally good."

Samuel Strickland.
Twenty-seven Years in Canada West, or, the Experience of an Early Settler.
London: Bentley, 1853, pp. 203–4.

great detail of his experiences as a settler in southwestern Ontario and then north of Peterborough in what is now Lakefield. "Apple and plum orchards," he wrote, in *Twenty-seven Years in Canada West*, "should be planted as soon as possible, and well fenced from the cattle and sheep. The best kind of grafted fruit trees, from three to seven years old, can be obtained for a shilling a tree; ungrafted, at four shillings the dozen. The apple tree flourishes extremely well in this country, and grows to a large size. I gathered last year, out of my orchard, several Ribstone pippins, each of which weighed more than twelve ounces, and were of a very fine flavour."

Detailed information from the earliest years is sparse and, for the most part, available from informal sources only. "Records are very meagre, publications few, and it is through letters, an occasional diary or recollections of early settlers passed on in the

The first two Secretaries of the Fruit Growers' Association of Ontario were Delos W. Beadle (1861–85) and Linus Woolverton (1846–1914), seen here. Both were sons of early horticulturalists, and both made major contributions to the field. Beadle was the author of *Canadian Fruit, Flower, and Kitchen Gardener* (1872), the earliest gardening book published in this country. Woolverton has two books to his credit, *The Canadian Apple Grower's Guide* (1910) and *The Fruits of Ontario* (1914).

Library and Archives Canada E002344165

families, that we get a glimpse of fruit growing in the early days,"[19] wrote Linus Woolverton in 1910. The Woolvertons were among the earliest and most important growers in the Niagara Peninsula. One of the first mentions of fruit growing in the region can be found in an account of how the family's Grimsby property was acquired, written by Charles E. Woolverton, father of Linus: "About 1796 one John Smith sold Jonathan Woolverton, my grandfather, 200 acres of land for £40 York Currency and the said Smith gave five nat-ural apple trees to bind the bargain."[20] As early as 1860, Charles Woolverton was operating a fruit-tree nursery. In 1910, his son Linus wrote that some of the early trees were still producing paying crops:

"One of these landmarks, an immense Greening apple tree, still stands on the old Woolverton homestead near Grimsby, and its huge spreading top covers an area of ground more than 40 feet in diameter. This tree has been known to yield twenty barrels of marketable apples in a single season."[21] Linus too is an important figure in the history of fruit growing in the province, and became the second editor of the influential magazine *The Canadian Horticulturalist*, published by the Fruit Growers' Association of Ontario.

The Fruit Growers' Association of Upper Canada, as it was originally called, was founded in January 1859, with Charles

From the 27th Annual Report of the Fruit Growers' Association of Ontario, 1895:

Mr. Caston: "I believe it possible from my own experiments to furnish the necessary manure to an orchard without the use of barnyard manure at all. One of the most successful farmers in west Ontario considers clover the best sheet anchor of farming. In regard to the time of plowing under, we find that clover is in that state early in June. We have sufficient moisture in the soil. If we plow it under, then we find in August when the drouth is at its greatest, that we have the ground in the very best mechanical condition; and I will guarantee that you can find the moisture within an inch or two of the top where that clover is plowed under."

• • •

Harold Jones: "Of the two seedling apples shown on the table, I wish to draw particular attention to the one that is known in our sector as the Scarlet Pippin. This apple originated in the vicinity of Brockville, and has been pretty generally planted in the counties of Leeds and Grenville. The fruit is well worthy of consideration by the Committee on New Fruits, and deserves a place in the list for judges at county agriculture fairs, as it is in good demand on the Ottawa and other markets, and is often called for by the commission merchants."

Forty years ago [that is, 1867] the Ontario farmer found a ready sale for the fruit grown in his orchard in the local markets, and no part of the farm yielded a more profitable return for the money and labour expended. As new settlers came into the province they adopted the common practice of setting out trees. ... The varieties ... were selected with a view to covering the entire season ... from the early harvest to the late winter. ... The result was a great admixture and confusion of varieties but nevertheless there was an orchard planted on every farm.

A. McNeil.
Co-operation in the Marketing of Apples.
Ottawa: 1907, p. 5.

Woolverton as one of the founding members. Thirteen years later membership had risen to 1600. The minutes of these early meetings make for fascinating reading, as members shared information on new varieties and solutions to problems in the orchard. From the very beginning, Ontario apples were winning acclaim at international fairs. In his presentation at the association's meeting in 1895, the Ontario Agriculture College representative drew attention to this: "I have often asked myself whether it was really possible that at that great Fair [the World's Fair in Chicago], with such extraordinary competition as there was there in fruit, that this Province of Ontario should actually receive about thirty-five per cent more marks or points for its fruit exhibit than any state in the United States."

By 1880, records show that eighty-four apple varieties were being grown in Ontario. (The McIntosh, destined to become the most famous Ontario apple of all, was not yet even mentioned! Although it had been discovered early in the century, it was still only known locally.) During the following thirty years, apples became an important part of the economy of the province – for local use, for the production of cider, and for export. The sale of nursery trees was a lively business, and a canning factory had been established at Grimsby, with apple dehydrators under consideration.

The Wonderful McIntosh

The McIntosh story is an almost unbelievable tale of the most famous of the truly Canadian apples, an apple that came into existence as an accidental planting and went on to become one of the most popular apples in the world!

The first tree is believed to have sprung up in a second growth bush in southeastern Ontario early in the 19th century. It was one of a few scattered apple trees that were discovered in about 1811 by John McIntosh when he was clearing land to build a house. McIntosh had come to Canada from New York as a young man of nineteen in 1796. After settling along the St. Lawrence, he married Hannah Doran and moved to the township of Matilda in Dundas County, not far from Morrisburg. The settlement around his new homestead was known for a time as McIntosh's Corners, but has since been named Dundela.

John McIntosh was pleased to find apple trees already under-way on his new property and moved them to the plot he had chosen for his orchard. It seems likely that the trees had sprouted from an apple core or two that had been discarded – probably of the Fameuse variety. Overall, the trees produced an indifferent mixture of apples, with the exception of one special tree. From its

It was Hannah McIntosh who first took care of the orchard, including the original McIntosh seedling which became known as "Granny's apple."

branches came the most flavourful, shiny, red apples anyone in the district had ever seen or tasted. John was happy to give seeds from these delicious apples to all the neighbours but, not surprisingly since apple seeds do not breed true, the wonderful apples grew only on that one tree.

His wife, Hannah, as usual in pioneer families, tended the small orchard and the special apple became known locally as the "Granny Apple" or "Granny's Apple." At one time a neighbour suggested that the family name be recognized in the variety, and it became the "McIntosh Red." The McIntoshes had twelve children. Allan, born in 1815, was the one who took the most serious interest in the apples. In 1835, an itinerant farmhand explained to Allan that the only way to reproduce the exact fruit of the tree was by grafting a branch onto another root, and showed him how to do

The McIntosh has even been immortalized in computer history by the creator of the Macintosh computer, Jef Raskin. "I named it for my favorite kind of eatin' apple," he wrote, "the succulent McIntosh (I changed the spelling of the name to avoid potential conflict with McIntosh, the audio equipment manufacturer)."

it. Allan was soon grafting new trees of the McIntosh for the orchard, and eventually he established a nursery and began sell-ing the saplings all over eastern Ontario. McIntosh Red (later simply McIntosh) was rarely grown outside of eastern Ontario until 1900 (probably because of its susceptibility to scab). As new spraying techniques developed around the turn of the century, the McIntosh took off.

That McIntosh orchard no longer exists and only an his-torical plaque at the side of the road alerts travellers to the original site of the farmhouse. Nearby, at Smyth Orchard, a descendant of the original settler sells Macs, and displays historic photos and documents related to the history of the apple.

All the words of praise associated with apples have been applied to the popular "Mac": sweet, juicy, tangy, tender, crisp,

Allan McIntosh and the original McIntosh tree about the end of the nineteenth century. Fire had damaged the tree in 1894 but it continued to bear a few apples until 1908. Allan McIntosh died in 1899.

Cornwall Museum/Archives

fine-textured and flavourful. It is recommended as an apple to be used cooked and for cider or for sauce, but is best eaten fresh from the tree.

The McIntosh has been used extensively in crossbreeding experiments in attempts to make it more resistant to disease. Among its progeny are Cortland, Lobo, Nova and Macoun.

The original McIntosh itself, however, remains the most popular apple in Canada and one of the most popular in North America. And, just imagine, every tree growing Macs is a part, or a part of a part, of that original lucky find, the McIntosh Red that appeared in Dundela!

By 1893, after a false start at the Agricultural College at Guelph, the Department of Agriculture was "successful in establishing a number of trial stations ... at points all over the Province."[22] These were at the farms of prominent growers, with Linus Woolverton and Dr. Macoun, the Dominion Horticulturalist in Ottawa, playing leading roles. Those involved contributed to the experimental breeding of favourable new varieties. Research expanded in 1906, when M.F. Rittenhouse contributed a large grant of land at Vineland. The Department of Agriculture built a major research station here.

Various cooperative marketing and shipping organizations formed and disbanded during the early decades of the twentieth century. Growers remained preoccupied with the same problems as those experienced in other parts of the country, the increase in insects and diseases (Paris Green and London Purple were among the insecticides and solutions of sulphate of iron or lime with sulphate of copper were used for diseases and fungi), the need to produce more perfect apples, the undependable weather (disastrous frosts in 1856–57 and 1933–34), the influence of war and international tariffs, and the extension of the railways and the introduction of refrigerator cars. In the 1920s, many of these matters began to be dealt with on a national basis through the Canadian Horticultural Council, which came into being in 1922.

THE WESTERN COUNTIES

Today the major apple producers in Ontario, and in Canada, lie in the area bounded by Georgian Bay, Lake Huron and Lake Erie. It seemed that a trip to the orchards of the Goderich and Meaford areas would yield some interesting stories.

I drove through Huron County's peaceful, rolling farmland one early summer day with introductions to a handful of apple

Sorting apples in 1919
Sallows Collection, Archival and
Special Collections, University of
Guelph Library

growers in the area east of Lake Huron in my briefcase. I was looking forward to visiting Goderich, famous for its "cartwheel" design,
laid out by John Galt. In Goderich, the Huron County Museum
staff directed me to the Reuben R. Sallows Gallery, attached to the
Goderich Public Library. The gallery is home to a wonderful collection of photographs celebrating rural life during the decades
before and after the turn of the twentieth century.

The orchards in this part of the province began as small,
family enterprises, part of the mixed farming economy of the day
and have remained much the same, some shrinking in acreage over
the years, others developing into commercial enterprises.

Ed and Pauline Laithwaite are apple growers at Apple Park,
one of the most interesting properties in western Ontario, on
Highway 8 about a kilometre southeast of Goderich. The history
of the house, the orchard and the family are recorded in two small
local publications, *The Concrete Statues of Apple Park* by Ralph Smith,
and *Early Huron Houses* by W.E. Elliott. George Laithwaite arrived
here with his new bride Mary in 1895 at what was already an
established fruit farm, which he called Maple Leaf Farm. Although
he devoted himself to the orchard, at heart he was an artist who
took delight in working in cement and stone. The story is that he
created the statues and the other stoneworks that fill the landscape as a way of distracting himself from the bad times of the
Depression in the 1930s. Although his work has suffered from
weathering over the years, visitors are still fascinated by the fig-
ures from the Bible, history, legends, local wildlife and his own
childhood that have survived on the property. Ed Laithwaite still
runs the Laithwaite orchard on the farm's sixty acres (twenty-four
hectares), and sells his own apples and other produce (as well as
those of other growers in the neighbourhood) from the small

One of George Laithwaite's famous statues

outlet on the property. Like other growers he regrets the loss of the days when his grandfather, George Laithwaite, supplied sixteen to eighteen local stores with fresh apples every week. Ed believes that today most people don't know how good fresh apples can be unless they buy them directly from an orchard in the fall when they have been picked at the peak of their flavour.

I found Ivan McClymont in the home he has retired to in Clinton; until recently, he was the fourth generation of McClymonts to tend an orchard on the farm just outside the village of Varna. The orchard was a typical size for the region, between seven and eight acres (roughly three hectares), with twenty-three varieties of apples, chiefly King, Talmon Sweet and Snow (Fameuse). In recent years Idared had taken over from Spartan as the best "keeper." All his apples were retailed at the gate or at the Bayfield Flea Market.

Ivan remembers spraying the orchard himself with a forty-gallon bamboo pump in the early days and later with the easier

86

field sprayer operated from a tractor. Over the years the original trees were replaced by dwarf plantings that made for easier care and picking.

In the nearby village of Bluevale, a small but intriguing apple and pear tree nursery, Woodwinds, can be found. This is one of more than six hundred certified organic farms in Ontario. The owner, Shelly Paulocik, provides an interesting range of heritage and other rare apple varieties by mail on a choice of rootstocks that will produce dwarf, semi–dwarf, vigorous or extra hardy trees.

Next, I headed north to the countryside around Meaford on the south shore of Georgian Bay. For many years the apple–growing

Shelly Paulocik at work in the Woodwinds nursery in the spring, the best time to prune and repair damaged trees

Photograph © 2002 by Wolf Kutnahorsky

area between Meaford and Collingwood, although the most northern in the province, has been one of the most productive with about 4500 acres (1800 hectares) of apple orchards. The microclimate created by the moderating effect of the deep waters of Nottawasaga Bay and the protection provided by the Niagara Escarpment to the south make it perfect for apples. Approximately 160 commercial apple growers in the area produce up to 3 million bushels of fruit, about 25 percent of Ontario's total crop.

James Carson and his son, originally from Ireland, arrived at Cape Rich, which juts out into Georgian Bay north of Meaford, in the mid-1830s. They brought with them seeds and seedlings from farther south. According to one story, another early settler, David Doran, who had settled on the Cape in 1837 brought McIntosh Red scions from his brother-in-law John McIntosh's orchard to graft onto the trees in his new orchard.

By 1851, six orchards in St. Vincent Township were listed, including the Londry farm, now the home of Grandma Lambe's, the famous retail store just outside Meaford. The orchard, originally planted in 1926 by Mabel and Hartley Lambe, now produces a wide variety of apples including Macs, Spys, Idareds, Delicious, Snows and Mutsus. Grace, the daughter-in-law of Mabel and Hartley, began to sell her popular apple pies at the roadside stand which had been operating since the 1920s. Soon business expanded until four generations of Lambes are now working in the enlarged Grandma Lambe's fruit and gift shop, selling more than thirty-five thousand apple pies a year. The shop, named after Grace's mother-in-law, "the original Grandma Lambe," now has its own kitchen and operates year-round with a staff of twelve.

By the early twentieth century the apple growers were providing jobs for many in the region: Natives on the local reserve

Apple pickers, dressed in their best for the photograph. The original Grandma Lambe's husband is on the left (circa 1902).
Grace Lambe

The year 1991 produced a bumper crop of apples in the Meaford area. Growers ran out of bins and storage. Here at Barbetta Orchards, another three-generation family-owned operation, local crops were held until they found a market at the nearby juice plant.

Brian Gilroy, Barbetta Orchards

made the half-bushel willow baskets used by the pickers, local coopers manufactured barrels and cedar ladders up to 25 feet tall and, of course, the pickers supplied the labour. In the early days, apples were transported to the harbour at Cape Rich on Georgian Bay and from there they went west to Manitoba and east to England. Shipping by boat was later taken over by trucks and trains.

In 1918 an apple-drying evaporator was established at the grist mill in Clarksburg. The mill later became Golden Town Apple Products.

> At the Evaporator the apples were peeled, cored, trimmed and sliced as they were carried along on a moving belt. They were placed on a shaker screen to remove seeds and seed cases, then moved to kilns for drying. The apples were spread about eight inches deep over the wooden slat floors of the kilns. They were dried by the heat coming up from coke-burners underneath. This slow process took up to twenty hours. The coke had to be stoked every half hour. Next they were placed in heated rooms for two weeks for curing. Dried apples were sold to lumber camps and institutions.[23]

One hundred pounds of fresh apples made about ten pounds of dried apples. Cider, apple vinegar and apple butter were all produced locally.

It seems incredible, but with modern plantings, six hundred trees are now growing in an area that once held only twenty-seven. The Ontario Ministry of Agriculture, Food and Rural Affairs (OMAFRA) lists the province's top varieties, in order of importance, as: McIntosh, Empire, Red Delicious, Northern Spy and Idared. There are approximately seven hundred commercial growers in the province, with orchards averaging eight hectares

The "Orchard Crisp" symbol guarantees that the apples are grown in Ontario.

(twenty acres). OMAFRA divides them into six apple-producing districts: St. Lawrence Valley, Eastern, Georgian Bay, Central, Niagara and South-Western. They produce about 13.7 million bushels each year. The value (farm-gate value) to the growers is about $85 million. About half the crop is sold as fresh apples – marketed under the "Orchard Crisp" brand name through packing plants – at farmers' markets and roadside stands. Ninety percent of the remainder are processed to make juice, or for apple sauce, slices and pie filling. Ten percent are exported to the United States or the United Kingdom. ☌

FRED JANSON: THE PASSIONATE GROWER

Fred Janson arrived in Canada with his wife, Walda, in 1951. Although he had a full-time job with Neilson's creating interesting new ice-cream flavours, apples were the passion of his life and became his full-time employment after he retired at fifty-five.

Pomona Orchards in Rockton, Ontario, nurtured by the Jansons, was famous among apple growers around the world who benefited from grafts of the rare apples they grew. More than 240 different heritage varieties grew in the orchard, where forty geese kept the grass trimmed and the ground clear of fallen fruit.

In 1967, Janson founded an organization for North American Fruit Explorers (NAFEX). Through its publication, *Pomona*, its more than three thousand members continue to exchange information on growing fruits on this continent. Fred's own extensive library became the

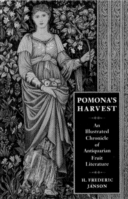

Pomona Book Store and in 1996 his own beautifully illustrated book, *Pomona's Harvest*, was published. In it he traces the history of apple lore against the social background of the times as well as providing an annotated bibliography of more than six hundred publications. The project was a twenty-year labour of love.

In 1987, Janson travelled to what was then the Soviet Union and wrote of the experience in the spring 1988 issue of *Pomona*, saying in part: "We found groves, now called florascapes, of wild trees typical of this Central Asian centre of origin of many familiar fruits. We walked along and through thickets of apple, pear, quince, apricot, almond, plum, walnut, persimmon, mayhaw and other unrecognized trees. Among the wild shrubby apples, we discovered veritable miniature replicas of Golden Delicious, Jonathan, Antonovka and Golden Russet, all with a crude crab taste." Fred Janson died in August 1999.

5

CROSSING THE PRAIRIES TO BRITISH COLUMBIA

Old Style Apple Pudding

"My grandmother's special recipe! Great alone or with ice-cream."

6 apples "Golden Delicious" peeled and cut up

½ cup water

Dash of nutmeg

⅓ cup white sugar

Place apples in square pan, add water, nutmeg and sugar.

Topping Mixture

¾ cup flour

¾ cup brown sugar

½ cup margarine or butter

Mix well and place evenly over apples and bake at 350°F for 45 minutes.

In Season: A Harvest of Okanagan Recipes from Davison Orchards & Friends. Vernon, BC: Davison Orchards, 1977, p. 47. Recipe by Rhea Cardinal.

THE PRAIRIE PROVINCES of Canada provide the apple grower with a number of serious challenges: extreme temperatures, a short growing season, inhospitable land in many places, a destructive sun in winter, and rapid changes in temperature, including that produced by the powerful winds of the chinook. On the positive side, as a result of the very long, cold winters, the trees suffer less from disease and insects.

Although no apples are native to the Prairies, even here it was natural for early settlers to try to create the home orchards on which they had been so dependent elsewhere. For this they needed extremely hardy trees. Crabapples and applecrabs (a term used principally on the Prairies for apples slightly larger than crabs – over five centimetres or two inches – and usually a cross between apples and crabapples) offered the best possibilities. The first successful attempts at developing an orchard were in the 1870s when Alexander P. Stevenson, originally from Scotland, settled near Morden, Manitoba. Through his experiments with Russian varieties, Stevenson was able to establish the beginning of an apple industry. He was not only successful on his own behalf with many of his apples winning prizes, but was also generous with advice and assistance to others. In Manitoba he became known as the "Apple King."

In 1888, the Morden Research Station was established as one of the branches of Ottawa's Central Experimental Farm. S.A. Bedford got the station underway, but its driving force was W.R. Leslie who remained its director for thirty-five years, from 1921 to 1946. An enthusiastic horticulturalist, Leslie was one of those responsible for developing the Prairie Cooperative Fruit Breeding Project. During his years at the research station, nineteen new apple varieties were introduced. One of these was the Mantet which, for a

Alexander P. Stevenson, "Apple
King" of Manitoba, 1916

Provincial Archives of Manitoba,
Jessup Collection 163 N11554.

Picking apples at the Morden
Experimental Farm, Minns Studio,
circa 1900

Provincial Archives of Manitoba 17 N3855

time, was popular from the Prairies to Nova Scotia, as well as in the northeastern United States.

The fruit-breeding project tested appropriate seedlings at a number of experimental orchards across the Prairies, including those at the universities of Saskatchewan and Alberta. Breeding apple trees is a slow process, but by 1976 the varieties Noret, Norcue and Norhey(22) were released, and in 1979, the more popular Norland, Parkland and Westland followed.

In Ottawa, Isabella Preston was working under the direction of the Dominion Horticulturalist W.T. Macoun. Preston was a noted breeder of flowering plants and one of the first women working in the field. Searching for a superhardy flowering crab, she crossed and recrossed *M. pumila* "Niedzwetzkyana" and the hardier *M. baccata*. The results, after years of work, were the beautifully coloured leaves, flowers and fruit of the rosybloom crabapple series.

Early tree plantings followed the settlers into the West before the turn of the twentieth century. Crabapples were planted at Fort Edmonton and were said to have survived on the grounds of the provincial government buildings there as late as the 1970s.

It is the crabapples (*Malus baccata*) developed especially for this climate that are treasured on the Prairies, in particular, the rosybloom series with its reddish purple colouring that affects everything from the flowers and fruit to the roots. There are many varieties, among them Almey, Selkirk, Garry and Rudolph (developed by the late Dr. Frank Skinner, the revered horticulturalist). Beautiful in both flower and fruit, they are especially popular with birds in the winter and spring.

In Saskatchewan, where the harsh weather is now beginning to be valued for its natural control against pests and diseases, the University of Saskatchewan has undertaken a program to

99

Rosybloom crabapple trees, developed by Isabella Preston in the 1920s, still bloom profusely at the Central Experimental Farm in Ottawa.

Photograph by Richard Hinchcliff, Friends of the Central Experimental Farm

develop apple trees suited to the climate. Under the direction of Rick Sawatzky, some local growers are beginning to produce organic fruit of high quality that Sawatzky sees as having huge potential for the future. At a time when conventionally produced fruit is flooding the market, organic apples are especially appreciated. For instance, near Radisson, northwest of Saskatoon, Craig and Yvette Hamilton have established a ten–acre apple orchard, Yoanna Nurseries and Orchards, the largest on the Prairies. With the advice of Rick Sawatzky, they have concentrated on two varieties developed at the university – Prairie Sun, which Yvette compares to Granny Smith as a multipurpose apple, "a really good keeper," and the as–yet–unnamed 18–10–32. Customers come to their U–Pick operation from as far away as Alberta and British Columbia.

BRITISH COLUMBIA'S UNIQUE CLIMATE

As with so many areas across the country, the early histories of British Columbia and the United States are closely interwoven, with the Hudson's Bay Company establishing forts on both sides of what is now the international boundary. When the Oregon Treaty was signed in 1846, the 49th parallel became the boundary west of the Rocky Mountains, and gradually, over the next twenty years, the company was forced to withdraw its forts to the north. The fur trade was to be the main activity there for some years, with little or no encouragement for agriculture. Then settlers began to arrive and cultivating food became a necessity.

There is a delightful story told of the first apple tree planted on the Hudson's Bay Company territory on the West Coast. In 1825 Sir George Simpson was sent to establish a Western fort as the headquarters for the fur trade there. He founded Fort Vancouver on the Columbia River about one hundred miles from the coast. Before he left London, he was entertained at a dinner held in his honour. As was often the case, apples were served and the woman seated beside Simpson dropped the seeds from her apple into his vest pocket saying, "Plant these in the wilderness when you arrive at your destination." Simpson probably forgot all about them but when attending a dinner at the young fort about a year later he came across the seeds. He turned them over to a Scottish gardener working at the fort, asking him to plant them. Some years later, the daughter of the Chief Factor at the fort was able to write about the result: "At first there was only one apple on the tree, and that everyone must taste. ... It was ripe; the only apple on the little tree. It was a great treat, for everyone had just a little slice. There were a good many it had to go round among."[24]

With the extension of the 49th parallel, Fort Vancouver became part of Oregon and the company moved its headquarters to Fort Victoria.

Before the middle of the 1800s, orchards were being established on Vancouver Island and along the Fraser Valley. Near Lillooet, an area warm in the summer but with severe winters, an Italian remembered only as Lorenzo is credited with planting the first orchard. In 1858 gold was discovered in Barkerville. Lillooet became an important stop for the goldrush miners looking for fresh provisions. Apples were a popular choice. In nearby Lytton, the first commercial orchard was established by Thomas G. Earl and in 1875 he was growing apples on three hundred acres. When the rush ended, sales dropped. This on top of the damage caused by the bitter winters of the period spelled the end of the orchard.

To the southeast, along the Similkameen Valley, was cattle-ranching country. The first settler along this trail, Francis Xavier Richter, arrived from Oregon with his family and a herd of cattle in 1864. After moving several times, the Richters ended up near Keremeos about twenty kilometres north of the American border. Here, in 1867, in the mellower climate, they established an orchard with trees brought from the United States. Later they added two more orchards, bringing in stock from Victoria. The Richters must have been highly successful growers because within ten years their apples began winning prizes at provincial exhibitions. In 1906 Richter apples won twenty-three prizes at the Provincial Exhibition at New Westminster and, four years later, a cultivar that Richter had developed, Banana, won a bronze medal in Vancouver. This success encouraged more local farmers to switch from herding and hunting to fruit and vegetable production. The work was labour-intensive and extra help was needed at harvest time. Chinese railworkers looking for work when the goldrush ended and the railway had been completed switched to harvesting. Before long, Keremeos became known for its roadside stands of fresh fruit and vegetables. As the harvests increased, the settlers began shipping produce west to Vancouver and east to the Prairies.

Another of the personalities connected with the early intro–duction of apples into B.C. was Hiram F. Smith, known as "Okanagan Smith." It is said that Smith planted 1200 apple trees on an acreage near Oroville, now south of the border in Washington State, in 1856–7. A few years ago a number of these trees, including Winesaps and Gloria Mundi, were still living.

The future heart of what would become British Columbia's famous fruitland, however, lay farther north along the shore of Okanagan Lake. It all began with the establishment of the Oblates' Immaculate Conception mission and Father Pandosy. Charles Pandosy was born in France in 1824. He first served at a mission

Father Pandosy
Kelowna Museum Archives #1886

in Yakima territory south of the U.S. border. Trouble between the American government and the Yakima Indians eventually persuaded the Oblates to move north to British Columbia. In 1859 Pandosy, accompanied by a small group of missionaries, established a mission in the Okanagan valley. It was the first permanent European settlement here.

In Penticton, where Pandosy spent much of his time, he is credited with planting the first apple trees and encouraging settlers and people of the First Nations to plant orchards. He has become an honoured figure in Okanagan history, and the site of the original mission is commonly referred to as the Father Pandosy mission.

The inland area stretching across the valleys of the Okanagan and the Similkameen–Nikola lakes receives little natural precipitation. In all other ways, including soil and temperature, it is perfect for apples and other fruit. In the late nineteenth century it became known as the Dry Belt and, if the nascent industry here was to be successful, irrigation would be essential.

Land grants for British military officers enticed settlers to the West in the mid–nineteenth century. Among them were Charles Frederick Houghton and the brothers Charles and Forbes Vernon who landed in Victoria in 1863. They headed for the Okanagan Valley, where cattle ranching was already well underway. Each staked 160 acres side by side and, by all accounts, these Irishmen spent much of their time gambling, horse racing, hunting coyotes and squandering vast amounts of money. In addition to spending time amusing themselves, the Vernon brothers built a grist mill on Coldstream Creek and planted a small orchard. Both properties eventually ended up in the ambitious hands of Forbes Vernon, who went on to become an MLA in the provincial leg–

"In broad general terms the interior of British Columbia may be described as an elevated tableland, deeply trenched by long, narrow valleys, which stretch parallel to one another from north to south. The valley of the Kootney Lake is the one that lies farthest inland from the Pacific. ... Proceeding from the Rockies towards the Pacific, the next valley is that of the Arrow Lakes, which also are fed by streams ... from the foothills of the Rockies. Then comes the Okanagan Valley, with its long and beautiful Lake, and beyond it, still farther west, the Similkameen-Nikola Valley, and finally the valley of the Fraser River."

J.T. Bealby. *Fruit Ranching in British Columbia.* Toronto: Macmillan, 1911, p. 31.

Young orchards at Coldstream
Ranch in the 1890s

Greater Vernon Museum and Archives #5029

The Nez Perce in traditional dress

Greater Vernon Museum and Archives #946

"One of the outstanding things I remember was an annual event: the migration of the Nez Perce Indian tribe. Practically the entire tribe came through the Hudson's Bay trail up to the Coldstream Ranch where they picked hops. And they moved their wives and families, hundreds of them, hundreds of pack horses. It was a real show. ... They looked like Indians of the traditional types – they wore the buckskins and moccasins and cowboy hats."

D. Mitchell and D. Duffy. *Bright Sunshine and a Brand New Country: Recollections of the Okanagan Valley 1880–1914.* Victoria: Provincial Archives of BC, 1980, p. 13.

islature, a position he held for nineteen years. The city of Vernon was later named in his honour. When he sold the property to the Earl of Aberdeen in the 1890s, it was renamed Coldstream Ranch.

John Campbell Gordon, the Earl of Aberdeen, had visited the Canadian West with his wife, Lady Ishbel, in 1890. They fell in love with the country and, before leaving, arranged to purchase a farm or ranch near Mission, with cattle, horses and farm tools included. They named the property Guisachan after Lady Ishbel's home in Scotland, and her brother, Coutts Marjoriebanks, took over management of the operation. They soon found that the return on the cattle didn't cover their investment and the crops did poorly on the arid fields, but the Aberdeens were not discouraged.

The following year they returned to Canada and visited the farm. In spite of the discouraging crops, they were delighted by one beautiful tree full of apples. Their plans to grow fruit on the land took hold. Before leaving this time, they made arrangements to buy the thirteen thousand–acre tract from Forbes Vernon.

In 1893, Lord Aberdeen was appointed governor general of Canada. Finally, in the fall of 1894, the family was able to travel west and see their new property for the first time. They were thrilled by its potential and spent a wonderful ten days there. Their huge hops crop had done well and harvesting was completed with the help of Salish workers from the surrounding area. Later, experienced Nez Perce Natives would come up from Washington State for the harvest – over the years they developed a routine of moving from harvest to harvest along the Okanagan.

Before the Aberdeens left, they had planted a hundred acres of fruit, chiefly apples, at each of the ranches.

During their stay in Ottawa, the Aberdeens travelled west for holidays every year. They were liberal social crusaders who contributed greatly to the community and became very popular with the people of the Okanagan. Lady Ishbel was involved in the cultural life of Vernon. She hosted musical entertainments and was involved in setting up a reading room and a cottage hospital. The Earl of Aberdeen was excited about the agricultural possibilities in the Okanagan. His planning and enthusiasm had a lasting effect on the future of the area as a major fruit centre.

A branch line from the CPR to Okanagan Landing had opened in 1892, and the following year a steamer, the SS *Aberdeen*, was making daily trips to Penticton at the south end of the 130-kilometre Okanagan Lake. This meant that good transportation for both people and goods was available and made it possible to open the land for settlement and agriculture. The whole valley was soon one vast orchard.

Lord Aberdeen was eager to encourage British settlers to move to British Columbia, buy property and develop the land for fruit crops. He became one of the first in the area to offer subdivided land to immigrants interested in investing in agriculture. A minor aristocracy was established as upper- and middle-class settlers from Great Britain were enticed to buy land. It became a home away from home for the new immigrants – Anglican churches sprang up, British newspapers were available, and the British accent was heard everywhere. Except for the busy times of the year in spring and fall when additional help was cheaply available, it was a leisurely life with all the activities they had known at home, including tennis, hunting and dancing.

The Aberdeens left Canada and the Okanagan in 1898, but they retained an interest in Coldstream Ranch until 1920. Their importance in the development of the Okanagan cannot be over-emphasized. In spite of this, the experience had been a financial

"The nature of this industry – small holdings of ten acres with intensive culture – tends to promote 'close settlement'; in other words, it is conducive to the establishment of small Fruit-Farming townships with all the social advantages attaching thereto; and, in consequence, it is interesting to note that, as I am informed, a considerable number of young men from our English Public Schools having, as they regard it, no prospects on this side beyond the office desk without expections, on leaving school, are being set up, after some training, as Fruit Farmers on the 'Dry Belt' of British Columbia."

"Note by Lord Strathcona," *Fruit Farming on the "Dry Belt" of British Columbia*. London: Times Book Club, [1909] 1912, unpaginated.

Aberdeen family

Greater Vernon Museum and Archives #11049

Coldstream Cider Display

Greater Vernon Museum and Archives #3404

"At Vernon we had the privilege of being shown the orchards, hops fields, and packing and storing houses of Lord Aberdeen's Coldstream Ranch, which has done more than probably any other to prove the practical possibility of commercial fruit-growing in British Columbia."

J.T. Bealby. *Fruit Ranching in British Columbia.* Toronto: Macmillan, 1911, p. 29.

disaster for them personally. In many ways they had been taken advantage of by almost everyone along the way, from real estate dealers to some of the managers they hired, and even by Ishbel's brother. All seemed to think the Aberdeens were wealthy enough to absorb any loss.

As the apple orchards expanded, the building of irrigation systems became more and more important and, by the late 1890s, provincial water records began to show a sharp increase in rights granted. The water systems included earth ditches, flumes, syphons and later concrete canals. Gradually the parched landscape took on a beautiful flush of colour as small orchard plots sprang up along the valley. The dry belt was greening, and by the beginning of World War I in 1914 all the major irrigation systems were in place.

As early as the nineteenth century, the difficulties of the Okanagan environment encouraged the farmers to cooperate. Their first step was the founding, in 1889, of the B.C. Fruit Grower's Association (BCFGA). The arid landscape wasn't their only problem. The valley was still without easy access to a major market until well into the twentieth century. Its north/south orientation was also perfectly designed to capture Arctic cold blasts and hold them until whole orchards were destroyed (as happened in 1949 and 1955).

Outside factors, such as worldwide economic changes, also had an effect on the success of the apple harvest – for good or ill. During World War I, the British embargo of 1917 (against imported goods, including apples) meant that an important market was no longer available to B.C. growers. On the other hand, a similar Canadian embargo against U.S. apples opened up the Prairies.

When World War I ended, governments looked for ways to help returning solders settle into productive areas of the country.

"The reliable delivery of water to orchards has also emerged as a serious issue in the 1920s as the wooden canals built by the land companies were proving to be of a sub-standard quality and in need of repair or replacement. In response, the Lands Project was to be equipped with a solid, concrete-lined ditch capable of carrying a high enough volume of water to meet the needs of all growers."[25]

Early irrigation consisted of a series
of pipes, wooden flumes and
ditches that carried the water from
creeks at a higher level to the
orchards.

Kelowna Museum Archives #3028

The ditch north of Oliver circa 1920.
Cement ditches replaced the earlier
flumes and meant that less precious
water was lost along the way.

Oliver and District Heritage Society Dr. D.B. Robinson
Memorial Archives #OLP.988.18.2

Picking apples in the Pridham
Orchard in Kelowna, 1910

Kelowna Museum Archives #2223

"I do not know whether you are
yet aware that a few weeks ago, at
the International Apple Show at
Spokane, Kelowna soundly beat
every important apple producing
area of the United States. We
entered in fourteen competitions,
and gained thirteen first prizes
and a minor prize. These included
nearly all the best prizes at the
show. ... We swept everything
before us in what many consider
the greatest Apple Show
ever held."

Secretary of the Kelowna Board of Trade. Quoted in *Fruit
Farming on the "Dry Belt" of British Columbia*. London:
Times Book Club, [1909] 1912, p. 59.

The orchard industry was highly successful at that time, so expanding the settlements into the Osoyoos area to the south seemed
an ideal solution. With government subsidization, seven hundred
orchard units of about ten acres were parcelled out. At the same
time immigration into what was promoted as a particularly
attractive place to live was expanding. "Both phases of settlement had been conducted with little regard for the natural

landscape, as marginal land, small orchard units and vagaries of the local weather would all play havoc with growers' attempts to make a living."[26]

In the decade following the war, new large orchards in the Okanagan came into their first harvest. Suddenly there were apples everywhere and nowhere to sell them at a decent price. The growers soon found that competing for the small market for their produce led to price cutting and losses for all. In order to survive, they needed to make changes. The BCFGA had originally been conceived to overlook the general health of the industry. Now, marketing became its major activity. In 1927 the association, through the B.C. government's *Produce Marketing Act*, set up a cooperative venture on behalf of Okanagan fruit growers. After some legal difficulties a "single-desk" marketing body, BC Tree Fruits, was created. All producers receiving government assistance were required to sell their crops through BC Tree Fruits. It, in turn, established Sun-Rype Products Ltd., which made available juices, pie fillings, bars, snacks and concentrates.

Although BC Tree Fruits served the Okanagan growers well for some years, for the Kootenay growers it marked the end of the era. The costs became too high for them to carry, and selling off the land in smaller lots to new settlers became more feasible.

"The 1940s proved to be the golden era of the fruit industry as an absence of competition created a false economy for all fruit in Canada."[27] But there was trouble ahead. Good times lulled the growers into believing that they could survive comfortably on smaller acreages and, since there was a fresh influx of would-be settlers looking for land, orchards were subdivided and acreages sold. By 1949 World War II restrictions on apple imports were removed and the fruit market was once more flooded. The final

"In the quest for stability, the BCFGA would be transformed both by growers and provincial legislation into a highly centralised, cooperative marketing organization, and an important component of public policy in this region."

Christopher John Garrish. "The Okanagan Fruit Growers and the Abandonment of Orderly Marketing." www.bcpl8s.ca/thesis.

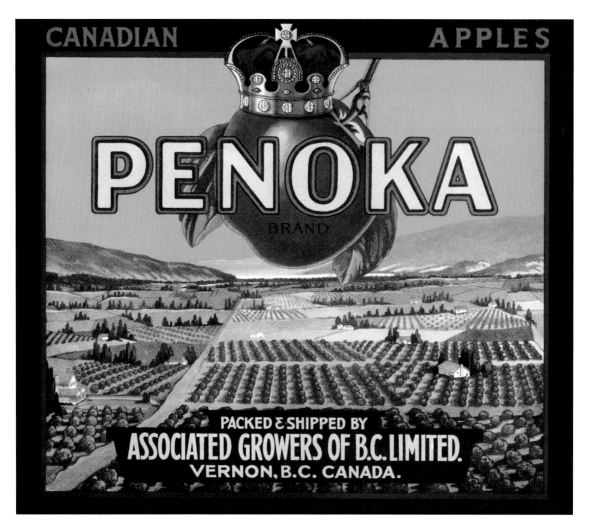

From the beginning, B.C. producers packed their apples in boxes rather than barrels. This meant fewer pieces of fruit were injured during shipping, which gave B.C. apples a good reputation in England. The boxes were identified by their decorative labels. These reproductions are a small sample of those once available.

Robert Davison, Davison Orchards

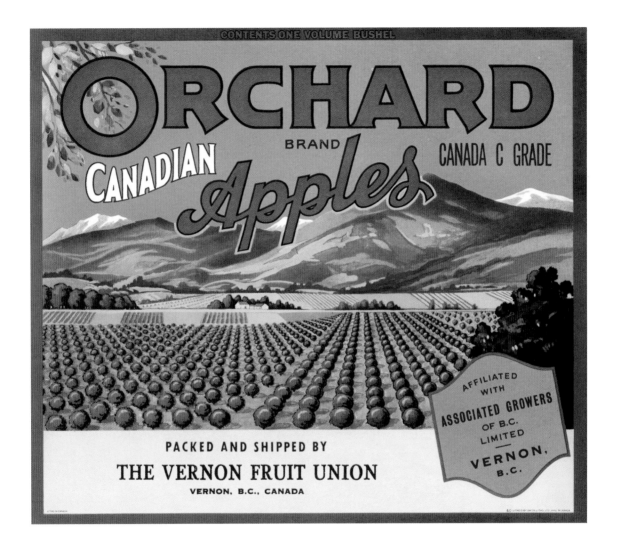

"In 1985, the commercial varieties sold by B.C. Tree Fruits were Red Delicious, McIntosh, Spartan, Golden Delicious, and in lesser quantities, Red Rome, Newtown, Winesap, and in very small quantities, Tydeman's Red, and Yellow Transparent."

R. Bruce Goett. *An Historical Survey of Okanagan Apple Varieties*. Kelowna: Kelowna Historical Museum, 1985, p. 18.

blow came that same year with a severe cold blast from the north bringing record lows that remained caught in the valleys for several weeks. Apple production dropped by almost 40 percent. To make matters worse, in the fall of 1955 another cold snap struck, revealing the inherent problems in the industry and the physical environment.

Growers now became disillusioned with controlled marketing and single-desk marketing. Society around them was rapidly changing. In 1962 the Trans-Canada Highway opened up the valley to a huge increase in traffic, giving growers the opportunity to sell their produce directly to customers (not allowed under the BC Tree Fruits' agreements). The larger orchards in Washington State, with their earlier harvests, were each marketing independently, giving Okanagan growers an example of another way to sell their fruit. New arrivals to the Okanagan found it difficult to see the advantages of single-desk marketing. Government assistance, originally only available to members of the BCFGA, was no longer restricted in this way. By 2001 membership in the association had dropped by about 80 percent. The BCFGA, so important to fruit growers of the Okanagan for decades, was unable to survive as a single marketer while the industry and the society within which it operated responded to the stresses of growth in the country.

SUMMERLAND

In 1914, the Summerland Experimental Station was established as part of the Dominion Experimental Farm system. Within two years the first orchards had been planted and their tree fruit-breeding program was underway. The apple-breeding program at Summerland (now the Pacific Agri-Food Research Centre) is

In the eight years from 1911 to 1919, B.C. apple production increased from 225,100 boxes to 2,500,000. The province was on its way to becoming one of the country's major producers of apples. One of the most important apples bred at Summerland was the Spartan, introduced in 1936. A hardy, crisp, juicy apple, it is one of the many descendants of the McIntosh.

120

Spectacular scenery on the way to the Okanagan

Photograph by Frank Wood

The Davison Orchards with Vernon below

Photograph by Frank Wood

VISITING AN OKANAGAN ORCHARD

Since I wasn't able to travel to B.C. to see the orchards myself, my brother, Frank Wood, who lives in Lions Bay north of Vancouver, offered to undertake the long, spectacular drive to the Okanagan. Phyllis Beardsley, a friend in Vernon, had suggested that Davison Orchards, a third-generation family-owned farm there, would be an interesting study. She was right. Although the farm specializes in apples, vegetables and fruit are grown as well. There are lots of other things going on at the Davisons': walking tours, orchard tours, wagon rides, hay rides, and visits to the farm market, the bakery and the gift shop. The Davison family welcomed Frank warmly and took an interest in the proposed book. He had a chance to see everything. "I can certainly vouch for the pie!" he later wrote – he's an expert on the subject!

Bob Davison, his son Tom and Tom's wife, Tamra, run the farm. Bob "is a terrific guy," wrote Frank, "who is a walking encyclopedia of apple growing and local history." He was also kind enough to send me a number of books on the history of apples in the province and on the Okanagan to speed my research.

Kelowna Land and Orchard is another popular family-owned farm in the area, where fresh fruit is available along with enough entertainment to keep visitors happy all day: walking tours, picnic tables (boxed lunches are available), a teahouse, fresh apple juice and relaxing hay wagon rides.

These are only two examples of the many other orchards, large and small, that can be found in the province.

responsible for carefully breeding and selecting fruit for quality, harvest season and hardiness in the Canadian climate. Entomological research aimed at protecting the trees has been another important area of study for the centre since that time. In 1921 R.C. Palmer and A.J. Mann joined the staff. Their work resulted in development of the Spartan apple, a popular cultivar with beautiful colour and firm, crisp, tasty flesh. Spartans have since been planted in north temperate zones around the world.

In the early years, B.C. orchards had escaped most of the damage caused by insects and disease, but by the 1920s codling moths, in addition to powdery mildew and fire blight, were causing

Tom and Tamra Davison, with some of the apples from their farm. The Davisons list eighteen varieties of apples from their orchards, including Transparents, Ginger Gold, Honeycrisp, Spartans and Mutsu.
Photograph by Tamra Davison

123

Spraying in the orchards, 1910

Greater Vernon Museum and Archives #3508

serious damage here too. Controlling these problems was of major importance. With the help of Summerland's pathologist Dr. H.R. McLarty, spray controls began to come into wide use.

By the 1930s apple farming, with the help of these scientific advances, began to develop into a significant commercial activity. Federal and provincial research facilities spread the latest information about the best methods for the orchard growers. Machinery and the use of chemicals replaced hand labour. New

124

In 2003 the Summerland research station promoted its work by inviting Canadians to name the latest apple introduced by the scientists there, a cross between Splendour and Gala. After more than 11,000 entries were considered, the winner, Daphne Biggs of Ottawa, named the shiny yellow fruit Aurora Golden Gala. It is described as "extremely crisp and juicy, firm and sweet" and should soon be available across the country.

Summerland Research Program

varieties and new rootstocks best suited to the province were introduced, and an emphasis on increasing the volume of fruit per acre was emphasized. "A 750,000 box apple crop in 1913 had increased to 2.5 million boxes in 1925 and 4 million by 1935."[28]

THE INDUSTRY TODAY

The British Columbia Ministry of Agriculture, Food & Fisheries reports that there are now about twelve hundred tree fruit growers

125

Organic Apples from Denman Island

Photograph by Kaj R. Svensson, Viewpoints West
Photofile Ltd. KS01-01

"'Yes, Mayne Island has lots of old orchards,' [Tina Farmilo] said. 'And it was once renowned for its King Apples, although there probably wasn't much to the talk about the island being the first place to grow apples on the coast. Maybe Saltspring Island,' Tina said. 'But not Mayne. The first apples in the Gulf Islands had come from such places as Nova Scotia's Annapolis Valley. They had arrived as twigs stuck into potatoes to survive the journey. The twigs were then grafted onto the islands' native crabapple trees, and that's how our first apple trees were born.'"

Terry Glavin.
Waiting for the Macaws and Other Stories from the Age of Extinctions.
Toronto: Viking, 2006, p. 193.

in the province of which up to five hundred are large commercial producers. The majority of these grow apples mainly in the three valleys, Okanagan, Similkameen and Creston, and produce about 275 million pounds of apples. A small but viable part of the industry practises organic farming. Four cooperative packers handle about three-quarters of these apples.

Most new orchards in the province these days are planted in the super-spindle style. This allows for a much higher yield from the land than in the past, with two feet between the trees and ten feet between the rows. There are up to twelve thousand trees per hectare, as compared to an earlier average of eighty per hectare. The provincial government encourages growers to switch to high-density plantings by offering financial subsidies to cover much of the cost. The higher density plantings are not only easier to harvest, but produce earlier crops.

Newer varieties (Gala, Royal Gala, Fuji and Ambrosia – a seedling discovered in the province) are gradually replacing the once all-important Spartan and McIntosh. The Okanagan Plant Improvement Company (PICO), owned by BCFGA, is dedicated to improving and distributing new varieties. ☙

6

THE PROOF…IS IN
THE EATING

"A IS FOR APPLE." Something every Canadian toddler learns at an early age, and the tree's bright, shiny, round fruit is familiar to us all. We see it in orchards, on roadside stands, in grocery stores, and in bowls and refrigerators in our homes. We have eaten apples in so many ways all our lives that a description of the fruit seems unnecessary. Apples are one of the most loved harbingers of fall, with varieties that ripen from midsummer until the first frost. Now, however, with modern refrigeration techniques, apples have become available all year long.

Round, oblong, conic or oblate, apples assume a number of similar but classifiable shapes. Colours range from green or yellow to orange and bright or deep red. Given a rub on a shirt sleeve, they reveal their bright, shiny splendour. Their attractive surface conceals much more than just a sweet, moist, crunchy interior.

In the ancient custom of wassailing, the farmer and his workers spent an evening drinking and toasting the best tree in the orchard with hot cider to encourage the next year's crop.

Wassailing the Apple Trees by Pauline Baynes, 1997, Bridgeman Art Library BAY 94084

129

Even squirrels recognize the taste
and value of apples, as seen in
this neat cache of fruit carefully
collected for future use.

Photograph by Bev Wigney
http://magickcanoe.com

The fruit, in spite of being about 85 percent water, is packed with many of the vitamins and minerals our bodies require and, even more important, are the phytochemicals such as flavonoids and polyphenols that they contain. They are rich in antioxidents (especially the skins). The skin of the Red Delicious and the flesh of the Northern Spy top the list. All are known to improve digestion (they are loaded with pectin) and to contribute to the health of the skin, eyes, bones, teeth and gums. And each apple contains only about eighty calories.

Perhaps "an apple a day" does keep the doctor away, or us away from the doctor's office. And it isn't difficult to meet that target with apples now available all year and no end to the ways they can be consumed: fresh, as juice, and in cooking in a myriad of ways. They are famous in pies, tasty in puddings, cakes, loaves, muffins, or even pancakes, and a good accompaniment to meats. They add moisture, sweetness and flavour to any dish.

Apple cider was a staple for human beings for hundreds, perhaps thousands, of years when it was sometimes the only safe drink available. That it can quickly become alcoholic (hard cider) was considered by many another benefit. Cider is a less significant part of our diet now, and is more widely available only after it has been pasteurized (soft cider) to extend its life and remove any alcohol. Then it is really just apple juice. True cider is still available at some orchards or through controlled outlets, and is currently making a comeback.

Some apples are popular because of their beauty, some because of their mouth-watering goodness eaten fresh, some because they are so useful in cooking. (Apples have even been used as the head of dolls by the Iroquois or for pioneer children.) Among the most popular apples in Canada are the McIntosh

"It was a universal custom to set a dish of apples and a pitcher of cider before everyone who came to the house. Any departures from this would have been thought disrespectful. The sweet cider was generally boiled down into a syrup, and, with apples quartered and cooked in it, was equal to a preserve, and made splendid pies. It was called apple sauce, and found its way to the table thrice a day."

Canniff Haight, writing about life in Upper Canada in the 1830s. *Country Life in Canada*. Toronto: Hunter, Rose, 1845, p. 22.

131

Chudleigh's orchard is open for fall apple picking, with the added enticements of corn roasts, tractor and wagon rides, apple cider and great pies from the on-site bakery. The orchard is located at Milton, Ontario, just below the Niagara Escarpment. They are most famous for their popular Apple Blossom pastry, available in many supermarkets.

Chudleigh's

(which many believe has never been bested) and the Red Delicious (probably for its looks and crunch rather than its so–so flavour).

From the hundreds of apple varieties readily available in the early decades of the nineteenth century, market forces that required wonderful–looking apples that shipped well meant that by the seventies only a handful were to be seen in supermarkets. In recent years, however, a few more varieties have once more become available. Each variety tends to be best in its own way, and, although many are available in abundance across the country,

When buying apples pay attention to the small sticky label on each: four digits indicate a conventionally grown apple, five digits beginning with "9" identify organically grown fruit, and five beginning with "8" means that the fruit has been genetically modified.

"... there were handy little machines that came on the market which, when mounted on the table by means of clamps, would speed the work. The operator had only to turn a crank handle and place one apple at a time on prongs, while the core was cut out and the skin was cut off by a sharp blade. The apples were trimmed and sliced and placed on screens above the cook stove to dry into rubbery chips." Similar devices are still available today.

Brent Almond. *The History of Meaford and Area Apple Industry*. Meaford, ON: Meaford Museum, 1985, p. 26.

Although only a few varieties of apples are available to Canadians in supermarkets, there are probably more than two thousand named cultivars growing throughout Canada. Expert estimates for the number of distinct varieties maintained around the world range from seven thousand to twenty thousand, many of them in national breeding collections.

different regions favour different apples – those that grow best in their climate or that were first developed there. Opinions differ as to which apples are overall best. Everyone has a personal favourite. Here are some of Canada's favourites and how they they can best be enjoyed.

Variety	Recommended Use
• Ambrosia – B.C.	fresh, salad
• Braeburn	fresh, salad, pie
• Crispin or Mutsu	fresh, cooking, cider
• Empire	fresh, salad
• Fameuse or Snow (Quebec)	fresh, cider
• Fuji	fresh, salad
• Gala	fresh
• Golden Delicious	fresh, salad, sauce
• Golden Russet	fresh, cider
• Granny Smith	fresh, salad, pie
• Gravenstein (Nova Scotia)	fresh, cooking, cider
• Honeycrisp	fresh, salad, sauce, pie, baked
• Idared	fresh, cooking, juice
• Jonagold	fresh, salad, sauce, pie, baked
• McIntosh	fresh, salad, pie
• Northern Spy	fresh, cooking, drying
• Red Delicious (B.C.)	fresh, salad
• Royal Gala	fresh, salad
• Russet	cider
• Spartan	fresh, salad, sauce, pie, baked

A recent book by Shahrokh Khanizadeh and Johanne Cousineau published by Agriculture and Agri-Food Canada, *Our Apples/ Les Pommiers de chez nous*, lists and describes the origins, quality and uses for more than two hundred cultivars grown commercially in Eastern and Central Canada (and much of the rest of the country). Many of these can be found in the fall at markets or roadside stands, as can older, heritage varieties.

Shahrokh Khanizadeh and Johanne Cousineau. *Our Apples/Les Pommiers de chez nous.* Saint-Jean-sur-Richelieu: Agriculture and Agri-Food Canada, 1998.

When it comes right down to it, all apples are delicious eaten fresh off the tree, after that it depends on personal taste.

Almost everyone has a well–loved apple dessert that can be made quickly and easily. In the following pages are a few recipes, new and old, that give some idea of the many ways apples can be used. ☀

Cooking With Apples

Apple Strudel

"This easy strudel is a satisfying finale to a meal. By combining dried fruit and a tart apple, no sugar is needed in the filling."

6 dried apricots

6 prunes

4 dried figs

½ cup port

2 Fuji apples, unpeeled, cut in chunks

2 tablespoons lemon juice

1 teaspoon cinnamon

½ cup fresh breadcrumbs

6 leaves phyllo dough

½ cup butter, melted

¼ cup granulated sugar

¼ cup ground almonds

Place apricots, prunes, figs and port in a small pot over medium high heat. Bring to a boil, simmer for 2 minutes, remove from heat and let sit for 10 minutes or until fruit is plump and soft. Drain the fruit and place in food processor. Add apples, lemon juice and cinnamon and process until everything is chunky. Mix in breadcrumbs and reserve.

Preheat oven to 375°F. Lay phyllo on counter and cover with a tea towel. Remove first sheet, brush with butter. Combine sugar and almonds and sprinkle about 1 tablespoon over butter. Top with second sheet of phyllos, butter and sprinkle with sugar/ almond mixture. Repeat with remaining sheets. Add any remaining mixture to apples

Place apple mixture about 2 inches from the long edge and 1 inch from the short edge. Fold in short sides and roll phyllo into a strudel shape. Brush with butter and cut 3 slits on top.

Bake for 25 to 30 minutes or until top is browned and mixture is cooked. Serves 4 with leftovers.

Lucy Waverman, *Globe and Mail* Food Columnist. www.lucywaverman.com.

Hot Spiced Apple Punch

2 cans (1.36 L each) apple juice

25 mL sugar

8 whole cloves

4 cinnamon sticks

5 mL whole allspice

2 mL nutmeg

Combine ingredients. Bring to boil and simmer 15 min. Strain. Serve hot, with cinnamon sticks, if desired. Makes about 2.5 L.

Apple Traditions the Modern Way.
Ottawa: Agriculture Canada, 1982.

Microwave Applesauce

6 medium apples

50 mL water

50 mL sugar

Dash cinnamon

Peel, core and slice apples. Place in glass baking dish, add water and cover. Microwave at full power for 6 minutes. Stir and continue cooking until apples are tender (1 to 6 minutes more, depending on variety of apples). Mash or sieve. Add sugar and cinnamon. Makes about 500 mL.

All about Canadian Apples. Ottawa: Agriculture Canada, 1982.

Apple Fritters

"Dip slices of reinette apples into batter, then place them one after another, with a silver spoon, in the frying butter or lard. When they have a good colour on one side turn them carefully; when they have browned equally take them out with a slotted spoon or a large wooden skewer. Powder them with sugar after they have drained well; then serve them."

Louis Liger. *Le ménage des champs.*

FRITTER BATTER

1 cup flour	Milk
3 oz cream cheese	OPTIONAL INGREDIENTS
Pinch of salt	sugar to taste
2 eggs	1 tbsp cognac or brandy
¾ cup white wine	

Sift the flour and salt in a large bowl, cut in the cheese; add slightly beaten eggs and wine and mix well. Thin with milk for a less dense batter. Sugar and/or cognac may be added if you wish; you may also sprinkle the tops with sugar or orange flower water. This batter is good for any food you may wish to fritter. It keeps well under refrigeration or can be frozen.

Hope Dunton and A.J.B. Johnston. *From the Hearth: Recipes from the World of 18th-Century Louisbourg.* Sydney, NS: University College of Cape Breton Press, 1986.

Apple Clafoutis

2 tbsp	30 mL	butter	3 eggs		
6 cups	1500 mL	pared sliced apples	2 tbsp	30 mL	apple brandy or rum
½ cup	125 mL	milk	¼ tsp	1 mL	baking powder
⅓ cup	75 mL	flour	pinch cinnamon		
¼ cup	50 mL	sugar			

In a frying pan melt butter over medium heat. Sauté apples until tender, 6–8 minutes. Arrange apples in a greased 2-qt (2 L) shallow dish or pie plate. Combine remaining ingredients in a blender and blend until smooth. Pour batter over apples, separating the slices with a fork to allow the batter to flow between. Bake at 350ºF (180ºC) for 50 minutes or until a knife inserted in centre comes out clean. Serve warm.

Makes: 6–8 Servings

Option: For cinnamon lovers: combine 1 tbsp (15 mL) sugar and ½ tsp (2 mL) cinnamon; sprinkle on top before baking.

Manitoba Agriculture and Food. www.agr.gc.ca/malus/nutrition_e.html.

Apple Cake

"A moist, sweet spicy cake – good for all occasions. It works with all kinds of apples. For a smooth cake, use an apple that cooks soft, such as a Spartan; for a chunkier cake, use an apple that keeps its shape after baking such as an Ida Red. Experiment with different varieties. I make this cake using the apples off the old generic apple tree in the yard. It produces an early-ripening, relatively soft, sweet apple."

2 eggs

1 cup sugar

1 tsp vanilla

½ cup vegetable oil

1 cup flour

¾ tsp cinnamon

¾ tsp baking soda

½ tsp nutmeg

½ tsp salt

½ cup chopped walnuts

2 cups peeled, chopped apples

Preheat oven to 350°F.

Grease and flour an 8-inch square baking pan.

Beat together the eggs and sugar, add vanilla, vegetable oil.

Sift together the flour, baking soda, spices and salt.

Combine with egg mixture.

Fold in chopped apples and walnuts.

Pour into pan and bake for 45–50 minutes or until it tests done.

Pamela Martin. *Thomasburg Walks*, www.thomasburg-walks.blogspot.com.

Baked Apples with Rum and Cider Sauce

6 large apples (Northern Spies are excellent for this recipe)

2 tbsp raisins

24 whole, blanched almonds

9 tbsp brown sugar

2 tbsp butter

⅓ cup water

1 tbsp rum

1 cup sweet cider

1 tbsp cornstarch

¼ tsp freshly grated nutmeg

whipped cream (optional)

Wash and core apples, leaving about ½″ of apple at the bottom to hold the filling. In each apple place 1 tsp of raisins, 4 whole almonds, 1½ tbsp brown sugar and 1 tsp butter. Score the skin at the top of the apple into sixths. As the apple cooks, it will open like a flower and not split unattractively.

Place the apples in an open, ovenproof dish big enough to accommodate them without touching. Combine the water and rum and pour in. Bake at 375°F until the apples are tender, about 30–35 minutes depending upon the variety (McIntosh take about 30; a firm variety like Northern Spy takes up to 50 minutes). Baste periodically with the pan juices. Remove the apples to a warm platter.

Shake the cider and cornstarch together in a jar. Combine with the pan juices (in a saucepan if the baking dish does not go on top of the stove). Cook until thick and clear. Stir in the nutmeg.

Pour some sauce over each apple. Serve the rest in a jug. Pass light cream or whipped heavy cream if desired.

Elizabeth Baird. *Classic Canadian Cooking*. Toronto: Lorimer, (1974) 1995, p. 103.

Spiced Apple Butter

"This is delicious on hot, buttered toast."

4 pounds apples (McIntosh, Cortland, Empire or Russet)

1½ cups apple cider

3½ cups packed brown sugar

2 tbsp lemon juice

1 tsp cinnamon

¼ tsp ground nutmeg

¼ tsp ground cloves

Cut apples into quarters. Slice each quarter into 4 or 5 slices. Place in a heavy pot; stir in cider. Bring to a boil over high heat, reduce heat and boil gently for about 15 minutes.

Ladle fruit and liquid into a strainer and push through, or put through a food mill. Return to a clean pot.

Stir in sugar, lemon juice and spices; cook over low heat, stirring constantly until sugar is dissolved. Bring to a boil, reduce heat and boil gently, uncovered for about 1 hour, or until thickened. Continue to lower heat and stir often until set (a small amount holds its shape when cooled).

Ladle into sterilized jars. Process jars in boiling water for 10 min. Let rest at room temperature until cool.

Yvonne Tremblay. *Prize-winning Preserves*. Toronto: Prentice Hall, 2001. www.yvonnetremblay.com.

Spartan Apple Potato Cakes

2 Spartan apples, peeled and shredded

1 lb (500 gm) russet potatoes, peeled, boiled and shredded

2 tbsp (25 mL) chopped fresh chives

3 tbsp (45 mL) canola oil

Salt and freshly ground pepper

Mound shredded apples in the centre of a clean kitchen towel, fold over towel to enclose apples completely, and twist ends to squeeze as much liquid from apples as possible. In a large bowl, stir together apples, potatoes, chives, 1 tbsp (15 mL) of the oil, and salt and pepper to taste. Shape apple mixture into 8 patties.

Heat remaining 2 tbsp (25 mL) oil in a non-stick skillet over medium heat. Add patties to skillet, in batches if necessary, and cook for 3 to 4 minutes on each side, until golden. Remove from skillet and keep warm. Makes 8 patties

Anita Stewart. *The Flavours of Canada: A Celebration of the Finest Regional Foods.* Vancouver: Raincoast Books, 2000, p. 28.

Apple Bread

"This moist bread is made with raw apple. If you're tired of banana or pumpkin bread, try it for a nice change."

½ cup oil

2 eggs

¾ cup sugar

1½ cups flour

1 tsp baking powder

½ tsp salt

1 tsp cinnamon

½ tsp nutmeg

2 cups peeled, coarsely chopped raw apple

½ cup chopped walnuts

Preheat the oven to 350°F. Grease a 9-by-5-inch loaf pan.

Using an electric mixer, beat oil, eggs, and sugar together until thoroughly blended. Sift the flour, baking soda, baking powder, salt, cinnamon and nutmeg together and stir into the egg mixture. Add the apple and nuts. Place in the prepared pan and bake at 350°F for approximately 50 minutes.

Nova Scotia Department of Agriculture and Fisheries, 2001.

Apple-Sumac Jelly

7 cups juice:

3.5 cups sumac juice

2.5 cups apple juice

1 cup commercial apple–cranberry juice (which had been sitting in the fridge), added to make up the 7 cups.

The proportion of apple to sumac juice was arrived at by the amount of each I had ready. The commercial juice was a whim I had. Different proportions and different bits of whimsy would probably work out as well.

JUICE

Sumac

To make the sumac juice: rinse the fruit clusters, cover with water, bring to a boil, boil gently for about 10 minutes, crush through a sieve, strain though a jelly bag, or three or four layers of cheesecloth in a colander. (Get a jelly bag!) You can add a little apple to check the cooking time: until the apple is soft. The juice will keep in the refrigerator for a few days.

Apple

Make your apple juice the same way – for small apples, cut off the blossom and stem end before cooking; larger ones, cut in quarters.

Jelly

Pour the prepared juices into a large pot, stir in one packet of pectin crystals, bring to a boil, add 8 cups sugar and boil hard for 1 minute. Take off heat, skim, bottle and seal.

Pamela Martin. *Thomasburg Walks,* www.thomasburg–walks.blogspot.com.

Stuffed Apples with Pork

*"An old German treat, easy and simple, to bake along with
a roast of pork or spare ribs."*

6 apples

1 cup breadcrumbs

1 onion

¼ cup raisins, soaked and
   chopped

2 crumbled sage leaves

Salt and pepper

Chop the onion and cook it in some dripping from the roast (or in butter), add sage, raisins, salt, pepper and crumbs and 2 or 3 tablespoons of drippings; brown all slightly. Core the apples and stuff them with the mixture. Put the apples around the roast, about three-quarters of an hour before the meat is ready to come out. Without a lid, keep roasting at 350°F til the apples are soft but not mushy. These are good with sausages too.

Edna Staebler. *Food That Really Schmecks.*
Toronto: McGraw-Hill Ryerson, 1968, p. 63.

Photograph by Peggy deWitt, Picton

NOTES

CHAPTER 1

1   Botanist Barrie Juniper led a team from Oxford University's Department of Plant Sciences to Alma Ata in 1998 and what he found there encouraged him to construct a possible history of the evolution of the apple from its early beginnings to the fruit we know today. *The Story of the Apple* by Barrie E. Juniper and David J. Mabberley (Portland, OR: Timber Press, 2006) tells this story and much more.

2   Quoted in Joan Morgan and Alison Richards, *The Book of Apples*. London: Ebury Press, 1993, p. 9.

3   Quoted in F.A. Roach, *Apple Production in England: Its History from Roman Times until the Present Day*. Reprinted from the *Journal of the Royal Agricultural Society of England*, vol. 125, 1964.

4   John Parkinson. *Paradisus Terrestris*. London: Humfrey Lownes and Robert Young, 1629.

5   F.A. Roach. *Apple Production in England: Its History from Roman Times until the Present Day*. Reprinted from the *Journal of the Royal Agricultural Society of England*, vol. 125, 1964, p. 51.

CHAPTER 2

6   *Voyages of Samuel de Champlain ... vol. III: 1611–1618*. Boston: Prince Society, 1882, p. 120.

7   F.G.J. Comeau. *Origin and History of the Apple Industry in Europe and America with Particular Reference to Old Acadia*. Halifax, 1934, p. xx.

8 Adolph B. Benson, ed. *Peter Kalm's Travels in North America*. New York: Wilson Erickson, 1937 [1770], p. 382.

9 Alice A. Martin. *All about Apples*. Boston: Houghton Mifflin, 1976, pp. 18–19.

10 Linus Woolverton. *The Fruits of Ontario*. Toronto: Ontario Department of Agriculture, 1914, p. 41.

11 *History of Fruit Growing and Handling in United States of America and Canada 1860–1972*. Pennsylvania: American Pomological Society, 1976, p. 177.

12 *Ibid.*, p. 178.

13 John Ferguson Snell. *Macdonald College of McGill University: A History from 1904–1955*. Montreal: McGill, 1963, p. 105.

14 S. Khanizadeh, Y. Groleau, J. Cousineau, R. Granger and G. Rousselle. "New Hardy Apple Selections from the Quebec Apple Breeding Program." *Acta Horticulturae*, 2000, p. 538.

15 C.G. Embree, ed. *Producing Apples in Eastern and Central Canada*. Ottawa: Agriculture Canada, 1993, pp. 14–15.

CHAPTER 3

16 Anne Hutten. *Valley Gold: The Story of the Apple Industry in Nova Scotia*. Halifax: Petheric, 1981, p. 101.

CHAPTER 4

17 Linus Woolverton. *The Fruits of Ontario*. Toronto: Department of Agriculture, Ontario, 1914, p. 53.

18 *Ibid.*, p. 71.

19 *80 Years: Highlights of History*. Toronto: Fruit Growers' Association of Ontario, 1940, p. 1.

20 *Ibid.*

21 Linus Woolverton. *The Canadian Apple Growers Guide*. Toronto: Briggs, 1910, p. 13.

22 *80 Years: Highlights of History*, p. 5.

23 Brent Almond. *The History of Meaford and Area Apple Industry*. Meaford: Meaford Museum, 1985, p. 26.

CHAPTER 5

24 David Dendy and Kathleen Kyle. *A Fruitful Century: The British Columbia Fruit Growers' Association, 1889–1989*. Kelowna: British Columbia Fruit Growers' Association, 1990, p. xiii.

25 Christopher John Garrish. "Okanagan Fruit Growers and the Abandonment of Orderly Marketing: Land Use Change, Single Desk Selling and the Coming of the Agricultural Land Reserve," thesis, chapter 2, "An Institution of the Interior," p. 4, www. bcpl8s.ca/thesis. I am indebted to Christopher Garrish for much of the background information here and regarding the development of the British Columbia Fruit Growers' Association and its related organizations. The complete story can be found on his website.

26 *Ibid.*, chapter 1, p. 6.

27 *Ibid.*, chapter 3, p. 1.

28 "History of Fruit Growing in the B.C. Interior," www. Livingland scapes.bc.ca. Vancouver: Royal BC Museum, p. 3.

SELECTED BIBLIOGRAPHY

Almond, Brent. *The History of Meaford and Area Apple Industry*. Meaford, ON: Meaford Museum, 1985.

The Apple in Ontario. Vineland, ON: Ontario Department of Agriculture, Bulleton 323, 1927.

Beadle, D.W. *Canadian Fruit, Flower and Kitchen Gardener*. Toronto: James Campbell, 1872.

Bealby, J.T. *Fruit Ranching in British Columbia*. Toronto: Macmillan, 1911.

Bennett, Jennifer. *The Harrowsmith Book of Fruit Trees*. Toronto: Camden, 1991.

Blackburne–Maze, Peter. *The Apple Book*. London: Hamlyn, 1986.

Brookshaw, George. *Pomona Britannica: The Complete Plates*. Koln, Ger.: Taschen, 2002.

Browning, Frank. *Apples*. New York: North Point Press, 1998.

Champlain, Samuel de. *The Works of Samuel de Champlain*, vol. V. Toronto: Champlain Society, 1922–6.

Chatten, Florence. *Brighton Apple Country*. Brighton: 1992.

Dendy, David, and Kathleen M. Kyle. *A Fruitful Century: The British Columbia Fruit Growers' Association 1889–1989*. Kelowna: British Columbia Fruit Growers' Association, 1990.

Dunae, Patrick A. *Gentlemen Immigrants: From the British Public Schools to the Canadian Frontier*. Vancouver: Douglas & McIntyre, 1981.

80 Years: Highlights of History. Toronto: Fruit Growers' Association of Ontario, 1940.

Elliott, W.E. *Early Huron Houses, Book One: Three on the Huron Road*. Goderich: 1965.

Embree, C.G. *Producing Apples in Eastern and Central Canada*. Ottawa: Agriculture Canada, (1899/E), 1993.

Establishing the High Density Supported Apple Orchard. Toronto: Ontario Ministry of Agriculture, Food and Rural Affairs, 1995.

Farrar, John Laird. *Trees in Canada*. Toronto: Fitzhenry & Whiteside, 1995.

Fidler, Isaac. *Observations on Professions, Literature, Manners and Immigration, in the United States and Canada Made during a Residence There in 1832*. London: Whittaker, Treacher, 1833.

French, Maida Parlow. *Apples Don't Just Grow*. Toronto: McClelland, 1954.

Fruit Farming on the "Dry Belt" of British Columbia. London: Times Book Club, [1909] 1912.

Fulton, A. *Packing Apples in Barrels and Boxes.* Ottawa: Department of Agriculture, 1926.

Garrish, Christopher John. "Okanagan Fruit Growers and the Abandonment of Orderly Marketing," thesis. www.bcpl8s.ca/thesis/.

Gendre, Sieur le. *The Manner of Ordering Trees.* London: Moseley, 1660.

Glavin, Terry. *Waiting for the Macaws and Other Stories from the Age of Extinction.* Toronto: Viking, 2006.

Goett, R. Bruce. *An Historical Survey of Okanagan Apple Varieties.* Kelowna, BC: Kelowna Historical Museum, 1985.

Goodrich, Norma Lorre. *The Medieval Myths.* New York: Mentor, 1961.

Guillet, Edward C. *Pioneer Days in Upper Canada.* Toronto: University of Toronto, 1933.

Haight, Canniff. *Country Life in Canada.* Toronto: Hunter, Rose, 1845.

Hall-Beyer, Bart, and Jean Richard. *Ecological Fruit Farming in the North.* Trois-Rivières, QC: Richard, 1983.

Heeney, H.B., and S.R. Miller. *Smithfield Experimental Farm: 1944–1985.* Ottawa: Agriculture Canada, Historical Series No. 26, 1986.

Hunter, Daryl. *The Kitchen Orchard.* CD-ROM. Fredericton, NB: Appleby Color Lab, 1998.

Hutten, Anne. *Valley Gold: The Story of the Apple Industry in Nova Scotia.* Halifax: Petheric, 1981.

Integrated Pest Management for Ontario Apple Orchards. Toronto: Ministry of Agriculture, Food and Rural Affairs, 1999.

Janson, H. Frederic. *Pomona's Harvest: An Illustrated Chronicle of Antiquarian Fruit Literature.* Portland, OR: Timber Press, 1996.

Juniper, Barrie E., and David J. Mabberley. *The Story of the Apple.* Portland, OR: Timber Press, 2006.

Khanizadeh, Shahrokh, and Johanne Cousineau. *Our Apples/Les Pommiers de chez nous.* St.-Jean-sur-Richelieu, PQ: Agriculture and Agri-Food Canada, 1998.

Knox, John. *An Historical Journal of the Campaigns in North America for the Years 1757, 1758, 1759 and 1760,* vol. I. Toronto: Champlain Society, 1914–16.

Lounsberry, Alice. *A Guide to the Trees.* Toronto: Briggs, 1900.

Lunn, Richard, and Janet Lunn. *The County: The First Hundred Years in Loyalist Prince Edward.* Picton: Prince Edward Council, 1967.

Macer Wright, David. *The Coxe's Orange Pippin: A Study in Cultivation.* London: Faber and Faber, 1957.

Macoun, John. *Co-operation in the Marketing of Apples.* Ottawa: 1907.

Martin, Alice A. *All about Apples.* Boston: Houghton Mifflin, 1976.

Mitchell, D., and D. Duffy. *Bright Sunshine and a Brand New Country: Recollections of the Okanagan Valley 1880–1914*. Victoria: Provincial Archives of B.C., 1980.

Morgan, Joan, and Alison Richards. *The Book of Apples*. London: Ebury Press, 1993.

Morse, Norman H. "An Economic History of the Apple Industry of the Annapolis Valley in Nova Scotia," unpublished thesis. Toronto: 1952.

New Apple Cultivars and Advanced Selections at Smithfield Experimental Farm. Trenton, ON: Agriculture Canada, Technical Bulletin no. 2, 1981.

Ormsby, Margaret A. *Coldstream Nulli Secundus: A History of the Corporation of the District of Coldstream*. Vernon, BC: District of Coldstream, 1990.

Pliny the Elder. *Natural Selection: A History*. London: Penguin, 1991.

Pomona [periodical published in various locations]: North American Fruit Explorers.

Roach, F.A. *Apple Production in England: Its History from Roman Times until the Present Day*. Reprinted from the *Journal of the Royal Agricultural Society of England*, vol. 125, 1964.

Roberts, Jonathan. *The Origins of Fruits & Vegetables*. New York: Universe, 2001.

Ronald, W.G., and H.J. Temmerman. *Tree Fruits for the Prairie Provinces*. Ottawa: Agriculture Canada, 1982.

Rosenstein, Mark. *In Praise of Apples: A Harvest of History, Horticulture and Recipes*. Asheville, NC: Lark Books, 1996.

Sanders, Rosanne. *The English Apple*. Oxford: Phaidon/Royal Horticultural Society, 1988.

Scott, James. *Huron County in Pioneer Times*. Goderich, ON: Huron County Historical Committee, 1954.

Seeds of Diversity [periodical]. Toronto: Seeds of Diversity Canada.

Silverstein, Alvin, and Virginia B. Silverstein. *Apples: All about Them*. Toronto: Prentice Hall, 1976.

Smith, Walter. *The Concrete statues of Apple Park: A Laithwaite Legacy*. Galt: 1995.

Snell, John Ferguson. *Macdonald College of McGill University: A History from 1904–1955*. Montreal: McGill, 1963.

Spafford, P.K. *As I Remember: Prince Edward County and Beyond*. Picton, ON: Prince Edward Historical Society, 1998.

Spangelo, L.P.S., R. Watkins and E.J. Davies. *Fruit Tree Propagation*. Ottawa: Department of Agriculture, 1968.

Stoat, Gilbert Malcolm. *Scenes and Studies of Savage Life*. London: Smith, Elder, 1868.

Strickland, Samuel. *Twenty-Seven Years in Canada West*. London: Bentley, 1853.

Thoreau, Henry David. "Wild Apples," *The Atlantic* (November 1862).

Todd, Sereno Edwards. *Apple Culturalist. A Complete Treatise for the Practical Pomologist*. New York: Harper, 1871.

Traill, Catharine Parr. *The Backwoods of Canada* (1836). Toronto: McClelland & Stewart, 1989.

——*The Canadian Settler's Guide* (1855). Toronto: McClelland & Stewart, 1969.

Upshall, W.H., ed., and D.V. Fisher, general coordinator. *History of Fruit Growing and Handling in United States of America and Canada, 1860–1972*. University Park, PA: American Pomological Society, 1976.

Webber, Jean. *A Rich and Beautiful Land: The History of the Valleys of the Okanagan, Similkameen and Shuswap*. Madeira Park, BC: Harbour, 1999.

Woolverton, Linus. *The Canadian Apple Grower's Guide*. Toronto: Briggs, 1910.

——*The Fruits of Ontario*. Toronto: Ontario Department of Agriculture, [1906] 1914.

Wynne, Peter. *Apples*. New York: Hawthorn Books, 1975.

Yepsen, Roger. *Apples*. New York: Norton, 1994.

INDEX

Overleaf: Tweed Memorial Park in winter